Quantum Frontiers

The Emerging Technologies Shaping the Quantum Revolution

Oliver Cook

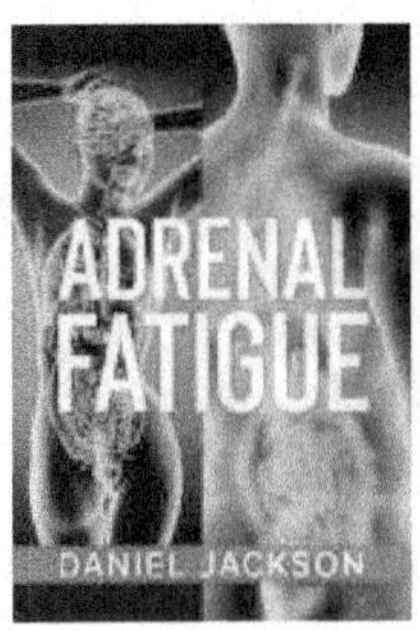

Take a look at more great books available from Rockwood Publishing

... **some for FREE!**

Just visit the link below:

rockwoodpublishing.co.uk

Contents

Chapter 1: Quantum Computing for Everyone

Making Sense of Quantum Mechanics

Welcome to the enthralling world of quantum computing. This realm of information technology is full of mystique, often painted with broad strokes of complexity and esotericism. But don't be daunted. It's not as unfathomable as it often appears. We're about to embark on a journey that will demystify quantum mechanics, and by extension, quantum computing.

Quantum mechanics underpins the operational principle of quantum computers. It's a branch of physics that ventures into the heart of the atomic and subatomic world, offering a set of rules that govern how particles like electrons, protons, and photons behave. At its core, it's about probabilities, superpositions, entanglement, and non-locality. If you're scratching your head at these terms, worry not, we'll uncover their meanings together.

Quantum Mechanics: The Basics

Quantum mechanics is like the code that runs the universe, governing the behavior of particles at the tiniest scales. In our everyday world, we're used to objects existing in one state at a time - a car is either parked or moving, a light switch is either on or off. But in the quantum world, things aren't quite so straightforward.

Here, particles can exist in a superposition of states - they can be in multiple states at the same time, only settling into one state when observed or measured. Imagine if your car could be both parked and moving at the same time, only deciding which state to be in when you looked at it. This is what quantum particles do - it's their version of normal.

The idea of superposition brings us to another bizarre but essential concept: quantum entanglement. When two quantum particles become entangled, their states are instantly connected, no matter how far apart they are. This means that the state of one particle will immediately affect the state of the other, even if they're light-years apart. This immediate, faster-than-light interaction contradicts Einstein's theory of relativity and is what Einstein famously dubbed "spooky action at a distance."

Quantum Computing: The New Frontier

The principles of quantum mechanics are directly harnessed in quantum computing. Conventional computers use bits to process information, where each bit can be either a 0 or a 1. Quantum computers, however, use quantum bits or "qubits". A qubit, thanks to superposition, can be in a state of 0, 1, or both at the same time. This means that a quantum computer can process a vast number of computations simultaneously.

Quantum entanglement plays a role here too. Entangled qubits can help perform complex calculations instantaneously. They're like a group of friends who, even when scattered around the world, know instantly what the others are thinking. It's this entanglement that gives quantum computers their potential for enormous computational power.

This power, however, is not without its challenges. Qubits are extremely sensitive to environmental interference, causing them to fall out of their quantum state in a process known as "decoherence". Scientists and engineers are still battling with this and other hurdles, like error correction and quantum programming, to make practical, large-scale quantum computing a reality.

Demystifying Quantum for the Everyday User

So, you might ask, what does all this mean for me? Do I need to understand quantum mechanics to use a quantum computer? Thankfully, the answer is no. The same way you don't need to understand the intricacies of semiconductor physics to use your laptop, you won't need a deep understanding of quantum mechanics to benefit from quantum computing.

Software developers and researchers are already developing user-friendly quantum programming languages and interfaces. These tools will abstract the underlying quantum mechanics, allowing you to reap the benefits of quantum computing without needing to grapple with the nuances of superposition and entanglement.

That said, having a basic understanding of quantum principles will undoubtedly give you an edge. It will help you appreciate the potential and limitations of quantum technology, and may even inspire you to explore the field more deeply. In an increasingly tech-dominated world, staying informed about cutting-edge technologies like quantum computing can only serve to enhance your professional and intellectual journey.

And so, as we venture deeper into the age of quantum, remember that this is a journey of discovery for all of us - researchers, engineers, and end-users alike. The quantum frontier is still being charted, its true potential yet to be fully unlocked. But one thing is certain - quantum computing is poised to revolutionize our world in ways we can barely begin to imagine.

In the coming chapters, we'll delve deeper into the practical applications of quantum technology, the ongoing challenges in the field, and the potential solutions to these challenges. We'll explore the societal implications of a quantum future, and most importantly, how you can participate in this thrilling quantum revolution.

Remember, the quantum world is not a distant reality, reserved only for physicists or computer scientists. It's here, it's happening, and it's for everyone. Welcome to the quantum frontier.

Unraveling Quantum Computing: Key Concepts Simplified

As we delve deeper into the quantum universe, the critical question that comes up is: how do we practically understand quantum computing? Our first step will be to simplify and demystify some of the key concepts of quantum computing. By the end of this chapter, you should have a clear understanding of these core concepts, how they differentiate quantum computers from classical ones, and why these differences make quantum computing so revolutionary.

Qubits: The Quantum Analogue to Classical Bits

In classical computing, bits are the fundamental units of data. A bit can either be a 0 or a 1, like an on or off switch. Quantum computing, on the other hand, introduces a new kind of bit: the quantum bit or qubit.

Here's where things get really interesting. A qubit, thanks to the principle of superposition, can exist in a state of 0, 1, or both at the same time. This allows quantum computers to handle a vast amount of information simultaneously, delivering enormous computational power. The tricky part is that when a qubit is observed, it collapses to either a 0 or 1, losing its superposition.

Imagine a world where every decision you make isn't merely a binary choice but a simultaneous exploration of every possible option, collapsing to a single decision only when the choice has been made. That's the essence of a qubit.

Quantum Superposition: Juggling Multiple States

A coin, when flipped in the air, shows both heads and tails, embodying a multitude of outcomes. When it lands, it "chooses" one—heads or tails. This scenario is a useful way to visualize quantum superposition, where a qubit can be in multiple states at once.

The principle of superposition leads to the exponential growth in computing power of quantum computers. A quantum computer with n qubits can process 2^n states simultaneously, an impossibility in classical computers. This quality enables quantum computers to solve complex problems exponentially faster than classical computers can.

Quantum Entanglement: A Spooky Connection

Another fundamental principle of quantum computing is entanglement. When two qubits become entangled, they form a linked pair, with the state of one instantly affecting the state of the other, regardless of distance. This "spooky action at a distance," as Einstein put it, allows quantum computers to process information in a deeply interconnected way that's simply not possible in classical computers.

The challenge lies in maintaining this entanglement, as it's very sensitive to environmental disturbance, a hurdle known as decoherence. Overcoming this hurdle is a key problem in the development of practical quantum computers.

Quantum Gates: Directing Qubits

Just as classical computers use logic gates to perform operations on bits, quantum computers use quantum gates to perform operations on qubits. However, unlike classical gates, which alter bits in a deterministic way, quantum gates manipulate qubits in ways that can only be described probabilistically.

Quantum gates direct qubits through a landscape of superposed states, creating a probability distribution that changes with each operation. The final outcome, observed when the qubits are measured, is a single result drawn from this distribution.

Quantum Algorithms: Harnessing Quantum Power

With the unique properties of qubits, quantum superposition, and entanglement, new types of algorithms have been created that leverage these properties for faster computation. These quantum algorithms could solve complex problems—from factoring large numbers to simulating complex chemical reactions—much faster than their classical counterparts.

Understanding these algorithms isn't an easy task for beginners. But don't worry, the current trend is towards developing higher-level quantum programming languages and software that will allow you to write quantum algorithms without deep quantum mechanical knowledge. Just like how you can create a website without understanding the binary code running in the background, you will be able to use quantum algorithms to solve problems, without needing to understand all the quantum intricacies involved.

Navigating Challenges in Quantum Computing

Quantum computing is not without its challenges. The superposition and entanglement of qubits are notoriously difficult to maintain due to their sensitivity to environmental disturbances. This issue of "decoherence" is one of the biggest obstacles faced in the pursuit of practical, large-scale quantum computing.

Additionally, quantum computing currently lacks the equivalent of a classical "compiler"—a tool that translates higher-level code into machine-level instructions. Developing robust, user-friendly quantum compilers is another crucial challenge facing the field.

Solutions for the Future

To tackle decoherence, researchers are investigating multiple paths, from improving the stability of qubits to developing error-correcting codes that can protect against decoherence.

On the software front, several tech giants and startups are developing more sophisticated quantum programming languages and compilers. They aim to simplify quantum programming to a level where even those without a deep understanding of quantum physics can write quantum algorithms.

It's also crucial to develop quantum algorithms that are resistant to errors, as quantum computers will be error-prone for the foreseeable future. Work is ongoing in this domain, with promising progress.

Bridging the Quantum Divide

Quantum computing has the potential to revolutionize many fields, but it remains a difficult concept to grasp. The key lies in education and awareness. Initiatives aimed at teaching quantum principles in schools and universities, as well as online learning platforms offering courses in quantum computing, are helping bridge this quantum divide.

Another aspect is fostering collaborations between physicists, computer scientists, mathematicians, and industry professionals. This cross-disciplinary approach could fast-track the development and adoption of quantum technologies.

Understanding the key concepts of quantum computing doesn't require you to be a quantum physicist. Just like you don't need to be an automotive engineer to drive a car, you don't need to be a quantum scientist to appreciate or eventually even to use quantum computing technology.

The quantum revolution is well underway, and we're all invited to participate in this exciting journey. As we continue to simplify, demystify, and uncover the world of quantum computing, rest assured that you're not alone in navigating this revolutionary frontier. Together, we're all part of this quantum exploration.

Quantum Breakthroughs: How They Shape Our Everyday Lives

As you delve further into the captivating world of quantum computing, a question may arise: "How do these quantum breakthroughs affect me?" The answer, much like the field of quantum computing itself, is multi-layered and profound. In this chapter, we'll unravel how quantum technologies have started to shape our everyday lives, provide potential solutions to problems we face, and explore the exciting future that lies ahead.

The Quantum Impact on Internet Security

One of the most immediate applications of quantum computing lies in internet security. The field of cryptography, which ensures the confidentiality, integrity, and authenticity of digital information, is on the verge of a significant quantum revolution.

Most of today's encryption systems rely on the difficulty of factoring large numbers, a task that classical computers struggle with. Quantum computers, however, can perform such tasks exponentially faster using Shor's algorithm. This means that many of our current encryption systems could become vulnerable in the so-called "quantum era."

While this may seem concerning, there's a silver lining. Quantum technology doesn't just pose a threat to security—it also provides the solution. Quantum key distribution (QKD) leverages the principles of quantum mechanics to create 'unhackable' security systems. In a QKD system, if a third party tries to intercept the quantum keys, it will disturb the quantum states of the system, revealing the eavesdropper.

Governments and corporations around the world are already investing heavily in QKD and other forms of quantum cryptography to prepare for the quantum future. As individuals, we'll benefit from these developments as they trickle down into personal cybersecurity solutions, providing an unprecedented level of data security.

Quantum Computing in Healthcare

The world of medicine and healthcare is also set to benefit hugely from quantum computing. From drug discovery to genomics, the potential applications are vast.

Drug discovery, a process which typically takes years and costs billions, involves searching through vast molecular spaces for potential candidates. Quantum computers, with their enormous processing power, could perform these searches exponentially faster, dramatically reducing the time and cost of bringing new drugs to market.

In genomics, quantum algorithms could be used to analyze DNA sequences more quickly and accurately than classical methods. This could enable personalized medicine, where treatments are tailored to an individual's genetic makeup, leading to more effective therapies with fewer side effects.

However, challenges remain. Quantum computers capable of these feats don't yet exist, and the development of quantum algorithms for these complex tasks is still in its infancy. But with the current rate of quantum advancements, these revolutionary changes in healthcare may be closer than we think.

The Future of Quantum and AI

Artificial intelligence (AI) and quantum computing are two revolutionary technologies that, when combined, could change the world as we know it. Quantum machine learning, an emerging field that combines these technologies, could lead to AI systems that learn faster and more effectively than their classical counterparts.

For example, these systems could more accurately predict weather patterns, optimize logistics in real-time, or even unlock new understanding of complex systems like financial markets or ecological systems. However, developing quantum machine learning algorithms and the hardware to run them are nontrivial tasks, and researchers are still in the early stages of this exciting journey.

From Breakthroughs to Everyday Impact

The promise of quantum computing is immense, but it's crucial to understand that we're still in the early stages of this technology. Quantum computers capable of surpassing classical computers—the so-called "quantum supremacy" or "quantum advantage"—are still in development. There are also considerable challenges to be overcome in maintaining quantum states and developing practical quantum algorithms.

However, the progress so far has been extraordinary, and the pace of quantum advancements is accelerating. Tech giants, startups, universities, and governments are investing billions into quantum research and development, leading to groundbreaking discoveries and technologies.

As end-users, we might not yet have a quantum computer on our desks, but the ripple effects of quantum breakthroughs are already reaching us—through more secure communication systems, advances in healthcare, and the development of powerful AI systems.

The quantum era isn't just about quantum physicists or computer scientists—it's about all of us. As quantum technologies continue to develop, they'll increasingly shape our everyday lives, offering solutions to some of the most complex problems we face and opening up unprecedented opportunities.

In this quantum journey, it's essential to stay informed and engaged. The quantum revolution is well underway, and we're all part of it. So as we continue to explore the vast potential of quantum computing in the coming chapters, remember that this isn't just a story about a distant, abstract technology. It's a story about our future—and it's a future that's looking increasingly quantum.

The Quantum Leap: How Quantum Outshines Classical Computing

As we journey further into the realm of quantum computing, one might wonder: "Why all this fuss about quantum? What makes it so special, and how does it outshine classical computing?" In this chapter, we'll unravel these questions by contrasting the capabilities of quantum computing with those of classical computing and shedding light on how quantum mechanics empowers us to solve problems that are out of reach for classical computers.

A Journey Beyond Binary

Traditional, or classical, computers operate in the realm of binary: every bit of information is either a 0 or a 1. It's remarkable how this simple binary system has enabled us to create a digital world of complex information. But this binary world has its limitations.

Quantum computing introduces a new fundamental unit of information: the quantum bit, or qubit. Unlike classical bits, qubits can exist in a state of 0, 1, or both at the same time, thanks to a property known as superposition. When we measure a qubit, it'll appear as either a 0 or 1. But in its quantum state, it can explore a multitude of possibilities simultaneously, delivering an enormous leap in computational power.

This ability to compute multiple possibilities at once enables quantum computers to solve certain problems exponentially faster than classical machines. That's the power of the quantum leap.

Entangled We Solve

Another quantum leap is made possible by the phenomenon of entanglement. In the quantum world, two qubits can become entangled, creating a bond where the state of one instantaneously affects the other, no matter the distance between them.

This 'spooky action at a distance', as Einstein famously put it, is not just a fascinating curiosity. It allows quantum computers to perform complex calculations in ways that are simply not possible with classical computers. It allows the computation to be done in a web of interconnected possibilities rather than a single, linear path.

Quantum Gates: Choreographing Qubits

While classical computers use logic gates to perform operations on bits, quantum computers use quantum gates to perform operations on qubits. Unlike classical gates, which transform bits in predictable, deterministic ways, quantum gates manipulate qubits in ways that can only be described probabilistically.

These quantum gates choreograph a dance of superposition and entanglement, driving the qubits through a complex computational ballet. The final outcome, observed when we measure the qubits, is drawn from the probability distribution that the quantum gates have created.

Unveiling Quantum Algorithms

In classical computing, we use algorithms—a series of steps or operations—to solve problems. Quantum computing brings in a new class of algorithms that harness quantum superposition and entanglement to deliver unparalleled computational power.

For instance, Shor's algorithm, a famous quantum algorithm, can factor large numbers exponentially faster than the best-known classical algorithm. Similarly, Grover's algorithm allows for faster searching of unsorted databases. These are just two examples of the kinds of problems where quantum algorithms outshine classical ones.

Quantum algorithms have the potential to revolutionize fields like cryptography, drug discovery, logistics, climate modeling, and financial modeling. They can perform tasks in seconds to minutes that would take classical computers thousands, even millions of years.

Quantum Challenges: The Road Ahead

Despite the remarkable potential of quantum computing, we are still in the early stages of realizing its full power. Practical quantum computers that can outperform classical machines—the so-called "quantum advantage"—remain a technological challenge. Achieving stable superposition and maintaining entanglement over long periods are non-trivial hurdles. But with global research and development efforts, progress is accelerating.

Making Quantum Leap a Reality

While there's no definitive timeline for when fully functional quantum computers will be commonplace, the race is definitely on. Tech giants like Google, IBM, and

Microsoft are competing with startups and research institutions around the globe to conquer the quantum frontier.

As we forge ahead, it's essential to have a robust understanding of both the potential and challenges of quantum computing. This knowledge will prepare us for the quantum era and enable us to harness this technology's power when it arrives.

In this journey, education, research, collaboration, and open dialogue are critical. Building a quantum workforce, fostering interdisciplinary research, and promoting public-private partnerships are steps toward making the quantum leap a reality.

Shining Bright: The Quantum Future

With its capability to process vast amounts of data and solve complex problems exponentially faster, quantum computing has the potential to revolutionize many sectors, from healthcare to finance to energy.

Yes, there will be challenges along the way, and yes, there is much we still need to learn. But the quantum leap isn't just about overcoming challenges; it's about unlocking potential—potential for innovation, discovery, and progress.

While we are only at the dawn of the quantum era, the potential of quantum computing to outshine classical computing is immense. And as we continue to explore this captivating field, it's clear that the quantum leap isn't just a scientific revolution—it's a revolution for all of us. The quantum future is bright, and it promises to shape our world in ways we can barely begin to imagine.

Exploring Real-World Scenarios with Quantum Simulations

Quantum mechanics, in all its perplexity, dictates the workings of the universe at its most fundamental level. It's a rulebook for particles, waves, and the very fabric of reality. Understanding this rulebook is essential for anyone hoping to navigate the quantum revolution. One of the most intriguing aspects of quantum mechanics, and subsequently quantum computing, is the potential for simulation. In this chapter, we'll dive deep into the world of quantum simulations, exploring their potential and illuminating how they could change our understanding of the world around us.

Why Quantum Simulations Matter

Simulations are a core tool in the toolkit of science and technology. They allow us to predict the weather, model the behavior of complex systems like global financial markets, and even simulate the inner workings of our brains. However, there are some phenomena, especially in the realms of quantum mechanics and chemistry, that are notoriously hard to simulate accurately with classical computers.

This is where quantum simulations come in. Because quantum computers operate on the same principles as the quantum phenomena they're simulating, they have a natural advantage. They can represent and manipulate quantum states directly, allowing for highly accurate simulations of quantum systems that are infeasible for classical computers.

Quantum Simulations: Bridging the Quantum-Classic Divide

Let's dig a bit deeper into what it means to simulate quantum phenomena. When we talk about quantum simulations, we're generally referring to one of two types:

1. *Digital quantum simulations* involve using quantum computers to simulate the dynamics of quantum systems. They use sequences of quantum gates to replicate the evolution of the quantum states they're simulating.
2. *Analog quantum simulations* involve custom-built quantum systems that are engineered to mimic the behavior of the quantum system you're interested in.

These two types of simulations provide different ways of exploring quantum phenomena, each with its own advantages and challenges.

Quantum Simulations and Material Science

One of the most exciting applications of quantum simulations lies in the field of material science. Materials with unique properties—like superconductors that carry current without resistance, or topological insulators that conduct electricity only on their surfaces—rely on quantum phenomena that are incredibly challenging to simulate with classical computers.

Quantum simulations could unlock a deeper understanding of these materials, leading to the discovery of new materials with tailored properties. This could revolutionize a range of industries, from electronics to renewable energy.

Imagine a world with batteries that charge in seconds and last for weeks, solar cells as efficient as photosynthesis, or superconductors that work at room temperature. These are the kinds of breakthroughs that quantum simulations could make possible.

Quantum Simulations in Chemistry

In the realm of chemistry, quantum simulations hold the potential to revolutionize everything from drug discovery to environmental sustainability. Quantum simulations can model molecular structures and reactions with high accuracy, providing valuable insights into chemical behavior.

Such simulations could dramatically accelerate the design of new drugs, reducing the time, cost, and risk of pharmaceutical research. They could also aid in the design of new catalysts—substances that speed up chemical reactions—for processes like carbon capture and storage, helping to combat climate change.

Challenges in Quantum Simulations

As promising as quantum simulations are, there are considerable challenges to overcome. Quantum systems are prone to errors and noise, and correcting these errors requires complex algorithms and additional qubits—resources that are scarce in today's quantum computers.

Moreover, designing quantum simulations that accurately reflect the real-world systems they're meant to mimic is a monumental task. It requires not just an understanding of quantum mechanics, but also of the system being simulated.

Building the Quantum Future with Simulations

Despite these challenges, the potential benefits of quantum simulations are too significant to ignore. They could enable breakthroughs in a range of fields, solving complex problems that are currently beyond our reach.

Moreover, they offer a way for us to explore and understand the quantum world on a deeper level, shedding light on the strange and counterintuitive phenomena that govern the universe on its smallest scales.

Whether you're a scientist trying to design a new material, a doctor looking for a new treatment, or just a curious individual trying to understand the quantum world, quantum simulations offer a powerful new tool to explore, experiment, and innovate.

As we continue this quantum journey, it's clear that quantum simulations aren't just about solving specific, practical problems—they're about expanding our horizons, pushing the boundaries of what's possible, and propelling us into a future where the weird and wonderful rules of quantum mechanics are a part of our everyday lives.

In the end, quantum simulations remind us that the quantum revolution isn't just about faster computers or more secure communication—it's about using the principles of quantum mechanics to understand and shape the world around us in ways we never thought possible. And that's a journey worth embarking on.

Chapter 2: Quantum Tech and Our Safety

Quantum Codes: How They Reinforce Cybersecurity

In our interconnected world, cybersecurity has become a paramount concern. The advent of quantum computing brings with it both challenges and opportunities for this critical field. Quantum computers have the potential to break traditional encryption algorithms, which could compromise the security of almost all current digital communication. But, on the flip side, quantum mechanics also offers new ways to secure our data, leading to the fascinating field of quantum cryptography.

Understanding Quantum Threats

To comprehend the role of quantum computing in cybersecurity, it's essential to understand its potential threat. Classical encryption algorithms, like RSA and ECC, rely on the computational difficulty of factoring large numbers into primes or finding the logarithm of a random elliptic curve point with respect to a known base point—problems that classical computers can't solve efficiently.

However, quantum computers, leveraging the principles of superposition and entanglement, could theoretically solve these problems more efficiently, breaking these encryption schemes. This potential future, where existing encryption methods become obsolete, is known as 'quantum apocalypse' in cybersecurity circles.

Embracing Quantum Cryptography

However, all is not lost. The same principles that could allow quantum computers to break classical codes also provide a foundation for new, more secure forms of encryption—welcome to the world of quantum cryptography.

The most famous quantum cryptographic protocol is Quantum Key Distribution (QKD). QKD leverages the properties of quantum mechanics to create and distribute encryption keys in such a way that any attempt to intercept or eavesdrop on the key would be immediately noticeable. The idea is based on the Heisenberg Uncertainty Principle, which, in essence, states that you can't measure a quantum system without disturbing it.

How Quantum Key Distribution Works

Let's break down how a simple form of QKD, known as BB84 after its inventors Bennett and Brassard and its inception year, 1984, works:

1. Alice, who wants to send a secure message to Bob, starts by randomly generating a sequence of bits (0s and 1s).

2. For each bit, she randomly chooses to encode it in one of two bases (say, the rectilinear or the diagonal) and sends it over a quantum channel (like a fiber-optic cable) to Bob.

3. Bob randomly chooses a basis to measure each bit. If he chooses the same basis Alice used to encode the bit, he'll correctly determine its value. If not, he'll get a random result.

4. After Bob has measured all the bits, Alice reveals which bases she used to encode them, and they discard any bits where Bob used the wrong basis.

5. What's left is a shared secret key that they can use to encrypt and decrypt messages.

Why Quantum Keys are Secure

The beauty of QKD is that any eavesdropper trying to intercept the key would necessarily disturb it, alerting Alice and Bob to the intrusion. Furthermore, thanks to the no-cloning theorem of quantum mechanics, it's impossible for an eavesdropper to make perfect copies of the quantum states encoding the key.

Quantum Cryptography Beyond Key Distribution

While QKD is the most developed application of quantum cryptography, it's far from the only one. Quantum money, quantum secret sharing, and device-independent quantum cryptography are just some of the other areas where the principles of quantum mechanics are being used to enhance security.

Quantum Cybersecurity Challenges

Despite the exciting potential of quantum cryptography, there are significant challenges to overcome. Practical issues like loss of photons in transmission and noise in quantum states can limit the effective range of QKD. However, techniques like quantum repeaters and satellite-based QKD are being developed to mitigate these problems.

Moreover, implementing quantum cryptography requires significant infrastructure changes. Quantum-safe hybrid systems, which use both classical and quantum cryptographic techniques, are seen as a transitional solution, offering improved security while the quantum infrastructure is built.

Quantum Future: Safer and Secure

Despite the challenges, quantum cryptography presents an exciting way forward in the face of the potential quantum threat to classical encryption methods. As quantum computing technology continues to evolve, so too will our methods of securing data against quantum threats.

Remember, quantum technology isn't just about faster computations—it's a game-changer for the very way we think about information and security. We're still in the early days of this quantum journey, but one thing's for sure: quantum technology has a significant role to play in shaping the future of cybersecurity. Quantum mechanics, once a theory reserved for physicists, is poised to become a crucial part of our daily digital interactions—keeping our digital communications secure in the quantum age.

Unseen Threats: Espionage in the Quantum World

In the realm of quantum computing, there is a kind of "arms race" happening. It's not the sort of arms race we saw during the Cold War with nations vying to have the most powerful nuclear arsenal. Instead, it's a race for supremacy in a world defined by zeros, ones, and the elusive quantum states in between. It's a race where the battlefield is not a geographical territory but the complex landscape of cyberspace, where hackers, governments, corporations, and everyday citizens all have a stake. The prize? Information. Control over it, access to it, the ability to secure it, and the power to decipher it.

Why Quantum Espionage?

Let's start by understanding why espionage is a concern in the quantum world. As I mentioned earlier, quantum computers can potentially solve problems exponentially faster than classical computers, including breaking most of the encryption algorithms we currently rely on to secure our online transactions, communications, and data storage. This capability makes quantum computers a prime target for espionage, whether it's state-sponsored hackers trying to steal technology and research, criminals seeking to profit from stolen data, or even corporations engaging in industrial espionage.

Moreover, as we start to build quantum networks and deploy quantum cryptographic solutions, new vulnerabilities may emerge that could be exploited. Hence, as we delve into the quantum world, we must remain vigilant to these unseen threats.

Quantum Espionage in Action

You might think quantum espionage sounds like something out of a science fiction novel, but it's closer to reality than you might think. In 2016, a group of Chinese scientists made headlines when they used a satellite to successfully perform a quantum-secured video call between Beijing and Vienna, demonstrating the feasibility of quantum key distribution (QKD) on a global scale. While this was a remarkable achievement, it also raised concerns about the potential for quantum espionage.

As nations and organizations race to develop quantum technologies, the risk of espionage increases. Quantum research labs could be targeted to steal research data, sabotage quantum experiments, or even pilfer prototype quantum devices. Quantum communication networks could be targeted to intercept quantum keys or manipulate quantum states. The list of potential threats goes on, and as quantum technology continues to evolve, so too will the tactics and techniques used by those looking to exploit it.

Mitigating Quantum Threats

Given these potential threats, how can we protect ourselves in the quantum world? Here are a few strategies:

1. **Quantum Cryptography:** As I've mentioned before, quantum cryptography, particularly Quantum Key Distribution (QKD), provides a way to secure communication in a way that any interception can be detected. Though it is not a catch-all solution and comes with its own set of challenges, QKD and other forms of quantum encryption are vital tools in the quantum security toolkit.

2. **Post-Quantum Cryptography:** While quantum cryptography is the ideal solution, the reality is that full-scale deployment of quantum networks is still a long way off. In the meantime, we need to secure our digital infrastructure against the potential threat of quantum computers. This is where post-quantum cryptography comes in. These are encryption algorithms that are believed to be secure against both quantum and classical computers. The National Institute of Standards and Technology (NIST) in the U.S. is currently in the process of evaluating various post-quantum cryptographic algorithms to standardize for future use.

3. **Security by Design:** As we design and build quantum systems, whether it's quantum computers, quantum networks, or quantum software, we must consider security at every step. This involves everything from physical security of quantum labs

to cybersecurity measures for quantum computers to secure protocols for quantum communication.

4. **Regulation and Cooperation:** As with any technology, there's a need for regulatory oversight to prevent misuse. This is particularly true for quantum technology given its potential impact on global security. Furthermore, international cooperation is necessary to set standards and norms for the use of quantum technology.

Towards a Secure Quantum Future

Quantum espionage presents a clear and present danger as we move into the era of quantum computing. But by understanding these threats and implementing robust security measures, we can mitigate these risks and harness the benefits of quantum technology.

It's important to remember that the quantum world, like the classical world, is not inherently good or bad. It's how we choose to use it that matters. While the potential threats of quantum espionage are real, so too are the potential benefits of quantum technology. By focusing on developing secure quantum systems and fostering a culture of ethical use of technology, we can help ensure that the quantum revolution leads to a safer, more secure digital world.

Quantum's Role in Making Our Data More Secure

In an era where our most personal information lives online, where businesses depend on secure digital transactions, and where governments rely on cyber-infrastructure for their essential functions, the security of data has become a concern of paramount importance. Amidst this reality, quantum technology presents a fascinating paradox. On one hand, it threatens to render obsolete many of the current cryptographic systems, which would leave our data vulnerable to quantum-armed adversaries. On the other hand, it offers new ways to secure our information that surpass what's possible with classical computing. Let's explore how quantum technology can make our data more secure.

Quantum Cryptography: Unprecedented Security Guarantees

The most direct way quantum mechanics can be applied to enhance data security is through quantum cryptography, which harnesses the peculiar properties of quantum particles to secure data.

One of the fundamental principles of quantum mechanics is that the mere act of observing a quantum system changes its state. This makes eavesdropping on a quantum communication channel not just detectable, but impossible to do without leaving a trace. This principle forms the basis of Quantum Key Distribution (QKD), the most widely developed quantum cryptographic protocol.

In QKD, the encryption key is shared between two parties using quantum particles, usually photons. If an eavesdropper attempts to intercept the key, their observation will disturb the quantum state of the particles, alerting the legitimate parties to the presence of the intruder. This allows for immediate action to be taken, such as aborting the communication or changing the encryption key.

This mechanism offers a level of security that is impossible to achieve with classical methods. QKD-based encryption, when correctly implemented, is secure against any eavesdropping attack, even those using more powerful quantum computers.

Quantum Random Number Generation: The Foundation of Secure Encryption

Secure encryption relies heavily on randomness. Encryption keys need to be truly random and unpredictable; otherwise, they can be guessed or reverse-engineered. In practice, however, generating true randomness is challenging with classical methods. Most random number generators used in computing are not truly random; they are pseudorandom, meaning they use algorithms to generate sequences of numbers that appear random but could be predicted if the algorithm and initial seed are known.

Quantum mechanics, however, offers a source of true randomness. Certain quantum phenomena, like the direction a photon will spin when measured, are fundamentally random. By measuring these phenomena, we can generate truly random numbers. These quantum random number generators (QRNGs) can provide a solid foundation for secure encryption by making encryption keys more unpredictable and harder to crack.

Quantum-Resistant Algorithms: Preparing for the Quantum Future

While quantum computers could break many existing cryptographic systems, they aren't the end-all and be-all of cryptography. Cryptographers are developing new algorithms that are resistant to both classical and quantum attacks. These so-called post-quantum or quantum-resistant algorithms are designed to run on classical computers but remain secure even in the face of a quantum computer attack.

While these algorithms do not exploit quantum properties themselves, their development is a crucial part of the quantum security landscape. They represent a kind of "Plan B" to secure our data in the event of a quantum computer becoming powerful enough to break existing encryption before large-scale, reliable quantum communication networks are a reality.

Quantum Clouds: Secure Quantum Processing

As quantum computers become more advanced, we're likely to see the rise of quantum clouds – cloud computing platforms that offer quantum processing power. This could enable secure quantum computing: performing computations on encrypted data in such a way that the cloud server never has access to the raw data.

This is a significant development because one of the biggest security risks with cloud computing is that the cloud provider – or a hacker who infiltrates the cloud server – could access and misuse your data. Quantum computing could provide a way to use the cloud while keeping your data secure.

Quantum Networks: The Next Frontier

Beyond securing data in storage and transit, quantum technology could also revolutionize the very networks over which data is sent. Scientists are working on creating quantum internet, which would allow quantum information to be transmitted over long distances. These networks could support secure quantum communication protocols like QKD, as well as novel applications like distributed quantum computing and quantum sensor networks.

The Quantum Security Paradox

Quantum technology presents us with a paradox. It threatens to undermine the security of our data by breaking existing encryption, but it also offers new and stronger ways to protect our data. It's essential, as we stand on the cusp of the quantum revolution, to invest not just in developing quantum computers, but also in harnessing the quantum world to safeguard our data against the threats of today and tomorrow. Quantum technology offers unprecedented opportunities for data security, and by embracing these possibilities, we can ensure that the digital age remains secure in the quantum future.

Quantum Diplomacy: Shaping Global Relations

As we stride further into the 21st century, a new type of diplomacy is beginning to take shape, influenced by the rapid advancements in quantum technology: Quantum Diplomacy. This term refers to the international relations and policy-making processes that revolve around the global development and deployment of quantum technologies. Let's delve into how the realm of quantum technologies is influencing geopolitics and international collaboration.

The International Quantum Race

In much the same way as the Space Race of the mid-20th century, nations worldwide are locked in a new form of competition, a Quantum Race, to be precise. The countries leading in this race, such as the United States, China, and several European countries, are pouring billions into quantum research and development, racing to unlock the vast potential that quantum technologies offer.

Much like the Space Race, the Quantum Race carries immense strategic significance. The country that manages to achieve a major breakthrough in quantum technology first would have a considerable advantage in areas such as intelligence gathering, military operations, cryptography, and economic power.

In this race, countries are not only racing against each other but are also racing against time. Quantum technologies, particularly quantum computing, pose a serious threat to our current cryptographic systems. The possibility of quantum computers breaking today's encryption techniques has given rise to the term "Y2Q" or "Years to Quantum," representing the time we have left to create quantum-safe encryption before quantum computers can crack our current systems.

Balancing Competition and Collaboration

While there is intense competition among nations, the field of quantum technology is also characterized by a high degree of international collaboration. Researchers across the globe regularly share findings and collaborate on projects, even as their home countries compete for quantum supremacy. This collaborative spirit is rooted in the scientific community's tradition, but it is also a pragmatic necessity: the challenges of quantum technology are so complex that they require a pooling of resources and minds.

But this balance between competition and collaboration is delicate. As the stakes in the Quantum Race rise, there's a risk that countries might become more protective of their research, leading to a reduction in collaboration. This could slow global progress in quantum technology and could create risks if one country achieves quantum breakthroughs without the proper safeguards in place.

The Role of Quantum Diplomacy

In this landscape, quantum diplomacy plays a crucial role. Diplomats and policymakers need to work together to ensure a level playing field in the Quantum Race, encouraging collaboration while preventing any misuse of quantum technologies. They must also foster a global consensus on norms and rules for the use of these technologies, much like the international treaties that govern nuclear technology or outer space.

Quantum diplomacy also extends to creating channels for cooperation, such as international research programs, student exchange programs, and shared standards and practices. These help to build trust, facilitate the exchange of ideas, and ensure that countries don't "go it alone" in a way that could be risky or destabilizing.

Challenges in Quantum Diplomacy

While the necessity of quantum diplomacy is apparent, implementing it effectively is fraught with challenges. For one, quantum technology is highly complex and esoteric. This makes it difficult for policymakers and diplomats, who usually do not have a background in quantum physics, to grasp the technology's nuances and potential implications fully.

Moreover, the speed of technological advancements outpaces the traditionally slow diplomatic processes. By the time an international agreement on a certain aspect of quantum technology is reached, the technology itself might have moved on.

Another challenge is that while the potential risks posed by quantum technology, such as threats to data security, are widely recognized, its potential benefits, such as ultra-secure communication, faster data processing, and breakthroughs in drug discovery, are less understood. This might lead to an overemphasis on the risks and underappreciation of the benefits, skewing policy debates and decisions.

Quantum Diplomacy: The Way Forward

Despite these challenges, quantum diplomacy is crucial in our quantum future. Policymakers, diplomats, and scientists must work together to navigate the complex landscape of quantum technology. This includes investing in scientific literacy for policymakers and diplomatic literacy for scientists.

Moreover, we must foster an international dialogue on quantum technology and its implications. This involves not just the countries at the forefront of the Quantum Race, but all nations, as the quantum revolution will impact everyone. This dialogue should be inclusive, incorporating voices from different sectors, including academia, industry, civil society, and the public.

Finally, we must remember that while quantum technology presents challenges, it also offers solutions. Quantum encryption can protect our data in ways that classical encryption cannot. Quantum sensors can monitor climate change more accurately. Quantum computers can help us design new materials and drugs. By focusing on these positives, quantum diplomacy can help guide us towards a future where quantum technology is used for the benefit of all.

Quantum Transport: Safeguarding Our Commerce and Trade

Trade and commerce form the lifeblood of our globalized economy, with goods, services, and information flowing continuously across borders. As these operations become increasingly digital, they also become more vulnerable to cyber threats. Enter the field of Quantum Transport. Leveraging the principles of quantum mechanics, this emerging domain aims to secure our commerce and trade in ways not possible with classical technologies.

Quantum in Trade: From Supply Chains to Financial Systems

At the heart of trade and commerce lie intricate supply chains, financial systems, and communication networks. These infrastructures rely heavily on data — tracking shipments, executing transactions, or communicating sensitive information. Quantum technologies can significantly enhance the security and efficiency of these operations.

A prime example is Quantum Key Distribution (QKD). QKD uses the principles of quantum mechanics to create virtually unbreakable encryption keys. These keys can protect financial transactions or confidential business communications from the threat of eavesdropping or data breaches. By integrating QKD into their operations, businesses can significantly bolster their data security.

Quantum Navigation and Timing

Quantum technologies can also impact physical aspects of trade, such as shipping and logistics. A particularly promising area is Quantum Navigation and Timing (QNT). Quantum sensors, such as quantum accelerometers and quantum gyroscopes, can provide ultra-precise measurements of acceleration and rotation. This can enable highly accurate navigation without relying on satellite-based systems, like the Global Positioning System (GPS).

Why is this significant? Satellite-based navigation is vulnerable to jamming and spoofing attacks, which can disrupt logistics operations. Moreover, in areas with poor satellite coverage, such as in the middle of the ocean or in polar regions, navigation can be challenging. Quantum sensors can operate independently of satellites, providing robust and reliable navigation in all conditions.

In addition to aiding navigation, quantum sensors can also provide highly precise timing. This is crucial for synchronizing operations in a supply chain or executing time-sensitive financial transactions. By offering resilience and precision, Quantum Navigation and Timing can enhance the efficiency and reliability of trade operations.

Quantum Computing in Trade Optimization

Quantum computing holds immense potential for optimizing complex trade operations. Trade and logistics involve numerous variables — routes, timings, costs, inventory levels, demand forecasts, and more. Finding the optimal solution amid these variables is a complex task that can stump even the most powerful classical computers. However, quantum computers, with their ability to process vast amounts of information simultaneously, can tackle these problems more efficiently.

For instance, quantum algorithms could optimize supply chain operations, minimizing costs while ensuring timely delivery of goods. They could also be used in high-frequency trading, rapidly analyzing market data to make profitable decisions faster than classical systems. While fully functional quantum computers are not yet a reality, the potential applications in trade and commerce are compelling.

Challenges and Considerations

While quantum technologies promise significant benefits for trade and commerce, they also bring challenges. Quantum technologies are still in their infancy, and considerable research and development are needed before they become commercially viable.

Moreover, there's the issue of quantum readiness. As with any technological transition, moving towards quantum technologies requires preparation. Businesses and governments will need to invest in infrastructure, training, and regulatory frameworks to fully leverage quantum technologies. There's also the need to maintain a balance between quantum and classical systems during this transition, ensuring business continuity and resilience.

The potential security risks posed by quantum technologies also need to be considered. Quantum computers could potentially break today's encryption systems, threatening data security. Measures need to be taken to transition towards quantum-safe encryption before this happens.

Navigating Towards a Quantum Future

As we navigate towards a quantum future, businesses, governments, and society at large need to understand the potential of quantum technologies and their implications for trade and commerce. As part of this, fostering international cooperation and dialogue is crucial, akin to the principles of Quantum Diplomacy discussed in the previous section.

While quantum technologies bring challenges, they also offer exciting solutions for safeguarding and optimizing our commerce and trade. By investing in research, preparation, and cooperation, we can ensure that we harness these technologies for the benefit of all. The quantum revolution is on the horizon, and its waves are set to transform trade and commerce as we know it.

Chapter 3: Quantum Tech and Society: A New Ethical Landscape

The Quantum Effect on Privacy: Redefining Boundaries

As we journey through the quantum revolution, we enter into a brave new world where traditional concepts of privacy and information security are being challenged and redefined. In this chapter, we're going to explore what quantum technology means for privacy and how it's transforming the ethical landscape.

Quantum technology, with its potent capabilities, holds the power to revolutionize various sectors – from cybersecurity to communications, computing to data storage. However, with this immense power comes the immense responsibility to navigate the ethical dilemmas it presents, particularly in terms of privacy.

Quantum Computing and Encryption: A Double-Edged Sword

The very basis of our online privacy rests on encryption algorithms that protect our data from prying eyes. Quantum computing, however, presents a paradoxical scenario. On one hand, it promises to deliver unprecedented levels of data security. Quantum Key Distribution (QKD), as discussed in previous chapters, allows for the exchange of cryptographic keys in a way that any attempt at interception fundamentally alters the information, alerting the communicators to the breach.

On the other hand, quantum computers, once they reach a stage known as "quantum supremacy" or "quantum advantage," hold the potential to break many of the encryption algorithms that protect our data today. This means quantum computers could potentially decrypt sensitive information — such as financial details, personal identification information, and state secrets — protected by current standards of encryption. This scenario is sometimes referred to as the "quantum apocalypse."

This dual-nature of quantum technology presents a unique challenge — how do we leverage the power of quantum technology for enhancing privacy, while also guarding against its potential misuse?

The Quantum-Privacy Paradox: Navigating the Path

Addressing this quantum-privacy paradox requires a multi-pronged approach. One of the primary solutions is developing and implementing post-quantum cryptography (PQC). PQC refers to cryptographic algorithms that, while they can be implemented on classical computers, are resistant to decryption by quantum computers. The development and standardization of PQC is a significant task that is currently underway, spearheaded by organizations like the National Institute of Standards and Technology (NIST) in the United States.

Simultaneously, we must continue advancing quantum-safe communication methods like QKD. Though it has limitations, including the distance over which it can be currently applied, research and development in this area can lead to more robust, scalable, and practical quantum communication solutions.

Educating stakeholders about the potential impact of quantum technology on privacy is another critical step. This includes not only businesses and governments but also the public. As quantum technology permeates society, a clear understanding of its implications can drive more informed policy decisions and promote responsible usage.

The Quantum Era: An Ethical Perspective

From an ethical perspective, the quantum era forces us to reassess our concepts of privacy and information security. As we transition to a world where quantum technology becomes mainstream, we need to have serious societal and philosophical discussions about the nature of privacy. What level of data security do we deem necessary for our digital society? How do we balance the trade-offs between technological advancement and privacy concerns?

Furthermore, ethical considerations extend beyond privacy. As with any disruptive technology, quantum technology could exacerbate social inequalities. For instance, quantum computing might initially be accessible only to large corporations or affluent countries, potentially increasing the digital divide. Addressing these issues requires thoughtful policies that promote the equitable distribution of quantum technology benefits.

The onset of the quantum era is a thrilling journey — full of promise, yet fraught with challenges. As we redefine the boundaries of privacy and navigate the new ethical landscape, the objective remains the same: harnessing the power of quantum technology for the betterment of society, while ensuring that we protect and respect the privacy rights of individuals. After all, technology is only as good as the ethical principles that guide its use.

Balancing the Scales: Quantum's Role in Economic Equality

In the tapestry of human history, technological revolutions have consistently acted as catalysts for change, shaping economic landscapes and driving societal transformations. The quantum revolution, undeniably, is poised to be a key determinant of economic progress in the future. However, as we herald this new era, it is crucial that we carefully consider how quantum technology could affect economic equality and what steps we can take to ensure a balanced future for all.

Quantum's Economic Disruption

As we discussed in previous chapters, quantum technologies hold the potential to disrupt a variety of sectors, from computing and cybersecurity to materials science, pharmaceuticals, and logistics. These advancements could trigger increased productivity, open new markets, and stimulate economic growth. However, just like the digital revolution led to the digital divide, there's a risk that the benefits of the quantum revolution might not be evenly distributed, leading to 'quantum divide.'

The Quantum Divide

The 'quantum divide' refers to the potential disparity in access to and benefits from quantum technologies. This divide could occur at several levels:

1. **Inter-country level**: Wealthier nations with more resources could gain a significant advantage over less affluent nations, widening the economic disparity between countries.

2. **Intra-country level**: Within a nation, large corporations with significant resources might gain access to quantum technologies much before smaller businesses, possibly exacerbating economic inequality.

3. **Individual level**: A lack of public understanding and access to quantum technology could lead to individuals missing out on potential benefits, while

some may also face increased privacy and security risks, as discussed in the previous section.

Addressing this quantum divide is essential to ensure that the quantum revolution leads to more equitable economic outcomes. But how can we achieve this?

Towards Economic Equality in the Quantum Era

Addressing the quantum divide and promoting economic equality in the quantum era require a holistic approach:

1. **Promoting international cooperation**: Quantum technology is a global challenge and opportunity that calls for international cooperation. Collaborative efforts can help pool resources, share knowledge, and ensure that more countries can participate in and benefit from the quantum revolution. Global standards and regulations could also help address security and ethical concerns.
2. **Encouraging public and private partnerships**: Partnerships between governments and private entities can help drive quantum research while ensuring broad access to the resulting technologies. Governments can offer grants, incentives, and regulatory frameworks that encourage quantum innovation while stipulating that the benefits should extend across the economy.
3. **Investing in quantum education**: To ensure that the benefits of quantum technologies are widespread, it's crucial that individuals understand these technologies. Investing in quantum education

at all levels—from primary schools to universities to adult education programs—can help demystify quantum technology and enable people to leverage its benefits.

4. **Developing inclusive quantum policies**: Policymakers must ensure that quantum technologies are used responsibly and equitably. This involves creating inclusive policies that consider the needs of all stakeholders, including those who might be disadvantaged by quantum technology.

Balancing the scales of economic equality in the quantum era is a daunting but necessary challenge. Quantum technology, like any other, is a tool; its impact—whether it exacerbates economic inequality or mitigates it—will depend on how we wield it.

With thoughtful strategies and cooperative efforts, we can ensure that the quantum revolution does not leave anyone behind but leads us towards a more equitable and prosperous future. The dialogue surrounding quantum technology's impact on economic equality is complex and ongoing, but it's a conversation that we all need to participate in as we stand at the cusp of this exciting new era.

The quantum revolution is not just about technology; it's also about people. As we continue exploring the quantum frontier, let's remember to do so with an eye towards creating a future that benefits everyone. After all, the most potent revolutions are those that lift all of humanity, not just a select few.

Making Quantum Tech Work for Everyone: Ethics in Practice

As the frontiers of quantum technology continue to expand, so too does our ethical responsibility to ensure that these advancements benefit all members of society, not just a privileged few. Quantum tech holds the potential to transform many aspects of our lives - from healthcare and cybersecurity to communication and artificial intelligence. However, these technologies also present new ethical challenges that we need to address to ensure that the quantum future is inclusive, fair, and secure for everyone.

The Quantum Ethical Landscape

The ethical landscape of quantum technologies is both broad and nuanced. Issues range from privacy and data security in the era of quantum computers to equitable access to quantum resources and the potential misuse of quantum technologies. Understanding these ethical challenges is the first step toward making quantum tech work for everyone.

1. **Privacy and Security**: As we've discussed earlier, quantum technologies, particularly quantum computers, could potentially break traditional

encryption methods, threatening digital privacy and security. It's essential to develop new encryption methods that can withstand quantum attacks, a field known as post-quantum cryptography.

2. **Access and Equity**: Quantum technologies could revolutionize industries, creating new jobs and opportunities. However, there's a risk that these benefits could be disproportionately available to wealthier countries and individuals with access to quantum resources, leading to increased inequalities.

3. **Misuse of Technology**: Quantum technology could be used maliciously or negligently, leading to harmful outcomes. For instance, quantum computers could be used to conduct cyber attacks, while quantum communication systems could be used to disseminate misinformation.

4. **Impact on Jobs**: The quantum revolution could disrupt traditional industries, potentially leading to job losses in some sectors while creating new opportunities in others. It's important to prepare the workforce for these changes to prevent increased unemployment and social upheaval.

Navigating the Quantum Ethical Minefield

Addressing these ethical challenges requires a concerted and proactive effort from all stakeholders – scientists, policymakers, businesses, and the public. Here are some ways we can ensure ethical practice in the development and use of quantum technologies:

1. **Regulation and Oversight**: Governments and international bodies need to develop regulatory frameworks to guide the use of quantum technologies. These rules should protect privacy, ensure security, and prevent misuse, while also encouraging innovation.

2. **Public-Private Partnerships**: Businesses, universities, and governments should work together to ensure the equitable development and distribution of quantum technologies. Such partnerships can pool resources, share expertise, and ensure a wide range of perspectives in the development of quantum tech.

3. **Education and Training**: Education is key to preparing society for the quantum revolution. Schools and universities should offer courses on quantum technologies, and businesses should provide training for employees. Public education programs can also help the general public understand the benefits and risks of quantum tech.

4. **Ethics in Quantum Research**: Scientists and researchers have a key role to play in ensuring ethical practice in quantum technologies. They should consider the ethical implications of their work and strive to develop technologies that benefit all of society, not just a select few.

Making quantum tech work for everyone is not a simple task, but it is a necessary one. As we continue to push the boundaries of what's possible with quantum technology, we must also push the boundaries of our ethical considerations. In this way, we can ensure that the quantum revolution brings benefits that are broad and inclusive, building a future that is as fair as it is technologically advanced.

Remember, the ultimate power of quantum technology isn't in the number of qubits or the complexity of quantum algorithms; it's in the ways these technologies can improve people's lives. By keeping ethical considerations at the forefront, we can guide the quantum revolution towards creating a world that's better for everyone.

The journey toward a quantum future is full of challenges, but it's also brimming with opportunities. With careful thought and concerted effort, we can navigate the ethical landscape of quantum technology, ensuring that these powerful tools bring about a future that's not just more technologically advanced, but also more fair, secure, and inclusive. After all, the most potent revolutions aren't just about changing the way we do things – they're about changing the world for the better.

Quantum Transformations: How It's Changing Our Lives Beyond Technology

Quantum technology, a seemingly esoteric discipline, is no longer confined to the realms of theoretical physics and sci-fi novels. It's a burgeoning reality with the potential to transform not only technology but also our everyday lives in ways we've yet to fully comprehend. Let's journey through the quantum landscape to understand how this emergent field can manifest changes beyond technology, from job market transformations, economic developments, to societal and philosophical evolutions.

1. The Job Market Transformation

One of the key areas of our lives where the quantum revolution is expected to make a significant impact is the job market. As quantum technologies advance, there will be a growing demand for quantum scientists, engineers, data analysts, and other quantum-related professionals. On the flip side, traditional sectors may see a shift as industries realign their operations around quantum capabilities.

In order to prepare for this transformation, it's crucial to invest in education and training. Countries, institutions, and organizations should foster quantum literacy, offering programs that equip individuals with the knowledge and skills needed in a quantum age. At the same time, it's also necessary to upskill workers in traditional sectors so they can adapt to the quantum-driven changes in their industries.

2. Economic Developments and Disruptions

Quantum technology's potential to outstrip classical computing in processing power could lead to immense economic transformations. New industries and services based on quantum technology could emerge, driving economic growth and reshaping existing market landscapes. However, these developments could also lead to economic disruptions, especially for industries heavily reliant on traditional computing.

One strategy to address potential economic disparities is to create policies that ensure equal access to quantum technologies and their benefits. Policymakers need to consider regulations and initiatives that promote equitable distribution of quantum resources and that guard against monopolistic practices in the quantum sector.

3. Societal Shifts: Quantum Communication and Security

The advent of quantum communication and quantum encryption technologies could lead to substantial societal shifts. Quantum communication, using the principles of quantum mechanics, has the potential to create ultra-secure channels of information transfer. This could revolutionize sectors such as banking, defense, healthcare, and any field requiring secure communication. However, this newfound quantum-enhanced security could also alter our societal landscape, raising questions about surveillance, privacy, and data control.

To navigate this complex terrain, societies might need to redefine their concepts of privacy and data security. Governments, technology companies, and individuals will need to strike a balance between harnessing the power of quantum technology and safeguarding fundamental rights and freedoms.

4. The Philosophical Evolution: A New Quantum Worldview

Finally, quantum physics, the very foundation of quantum technology, challenges our classical understanding of the world. Its principles of superposition, entanglement, and the observer effect force us to rethink our notions of reality, causality, and identity. Embracing quantum technology might mean embracing a new worldview that sees the world not as a collection of discrete, independent entities, but as a complex web of interconnected phenomena.

This philosophical shift can enrich our lives by offering a broader perspective that appreciates complexity, interconnectedness, and the myriad possibilities that quantum mechanics affirms. It could lead to a more holistic understanding of the world, influencing fields as diverse as philosophy, psychology, and even spirituality.

Quantum technology is not just about faster processors, secure communication, or efficient algorithms. It's about a transformative shift that extends beyond technology, permeating various aspects of our lives.

As we venture deeper into the quantum age, it's crucial to keep the dialogue about these transformations alive. This way, we can anticipate challenges, devise solutions, and guide the quantum revolution in a way that benefits all, not just technologically, but also economically, socially, and philosophically.

It's an exciting era, one that holds the promise of not just technological breakthroughs but also deeper insights into the workings of the universe and our place within it. As we navigate through this quantum transformation, let's remember to view it not just as a technological shift, but as an opportunity for societal advancement and philosophical growth.

In the final analysis, it's not just about how quantum is changing our technology, but about how it's transforming us, our world, and our understanding of reality.

The quantum revolution is more than just a leap in computational power - it's a leap in our collective consciousness, a leap towards a future where technology, society, and philosophy converge in the quantum realm.

Chapter 4: Quantum Tech: Reshaping Industries

Quantum Solutions in Healthcare: From Diagnosing Illness to Discovering Cures

As the world continues to grapple with healthcare challenges, we're now at the threshold of a promising revolution - a quantum revolution. From unveiling new pathways for drug discovery to unlocking a new era in diagnostics and personalized medicine, quantum technology stands ready to alter our healthcare landscape in profound ways. This transformation promises not only to enhance our ability to diagnose and treat illness but also opens avenues to discover groundbreaking cures.

1. Quantum Computing in Drug Discovery

The promise of quantum computing in drug discovery is almost unfathomable. To understand this potential, consider the fact that the human body is home to an estimated 20,000-25,000 proteins. The interactions between these proteins and potential drug molecules are so complex that exploring all possibilities with classical computers is nearly impossible.

However, quantum computing, with its enormous computational power, has the potential to explore this vast solution space effectively. By processing multiple possibilities simultaneously, thanks to quantum superposition, quantum computers can simulate molecular structures and interactions far more efficiently than classical computers. This will accelerate drug discovery, potentially saving millions of lives by fast-tracking cures for diseases that are currently untreatable.

For those tasked with making this a reality, it's important to invest in building robust quantum infrastructure and platforms that can handle these complex simulations. Collaborative efforts between quantum scientists, biologists, and medical professionals will also be key to ensuring these advancements translate effectively from the lab to the clinic.

2. Diagnostics and Personalized Medicine

Quantum technology's potential in diagnostics is twofold. First, quantum sensors, renowned for their exceptional sensitivity, can detect minute changes in the body that could signal the presence of a disease, possibly even before symptoms appear. Second, quantum computing, combined with AI, could analyze vast datasets of patient information, identifying patterns and insights that could lead to more accurate, early diagnoses.

Furthermore, this combination of quantum computing and AI could also facilitate personalized medicine, tailoring treatments to an individual's genetic makeup, lifestyle, and environmental factors. The challenge here lies in securing and managing this vast quantum of personal health data. Implementing quantum-safe encryption measures and robust privacy policies will be essential to ensuring this transformative technology can be trusted and accepted by individuals and society.

3. Quantum Imaging: Unveiling the Unseen

Quantum imaging techniques, such as quantum tomography and quantum illumination, could revolutionize medical imaging, offering unprecedented levels of detail and sensitivity. For instance, quantum tomography could potentially detect tumorous cells before they form a sizeable mass, vastly improving the chances of successful treatment.

Yet, the development of these techniques poses significant technical challenges. Scientists, engineers, and clinicians must work together to transform these quantum theories into practical tools. Alongside this, governments and institutions should foster an environment conducive to such ground-breaking research and ensure ethical standards are met during the development and deployment of these technologies.

4. Training Quantum Healthcare Professionals

Last but not least, the advent of quantum in healthcare will require a new breed of healthcare professionals – ones who are comfortable working with quantum technologies. This calls for an overhaul in medical education and continuous training for existing healthcare professionals. Initiatives should aim at integrating quantum sciences into medical curricula and creating lifelong learning opportunities for those already in the field.

The incursion of quantum technologies into healthcare is not a matter of if but when. As we traverse this quantum frontier, we must keep in mind that while quantum technologies can provide us with powerful tools for tackling healthcare challenges, their effective and ethical implementation rests in our hands. The onus is on us to create a healthcare system that leverages these advancements while ensuring privacy, fairness, and accessibility.

So, let's embrace this quantum revolution in healthcare – not just as scientists, engineers, or medical professionals, but as a society. Because, in the end, the goal of quantum tech in healthcare, like any technology, is to serve us, the people, making our lives healthier and our societies more resilient. Quantum technologies in healthcare give us a glimpse into a future where diagnosing illness and discovering cures could be more precise, efficient, and personalized. Let's strive together to turn this quantum vision into reality.

A Quantum Approach to Money Matters: Finance Transformed

The era of quantum computing is upon us, and its effects will reverberate through every facet of our lives, including the realm of finance. From optimizing portfolios to fraud detection, deciphering complex financial markets, and bolstering cybersecurity, the quantum revolution in finance stands ready to rewrite the rules of the game.

1. Portfolio Optimization in a Quantum World

The financial markets are complex, often chaotic systems, where the number of variables that can influence the success of an investment portfolio can be overwhelming. The challenge of finding the optimal mix of investments – or portfolio optimization – is a task classical computers struggle with due to its combinatorial nature.

However, quantum computers, with their ability to process multiple combinations simultaneously, present a promising solution. The inherent ability of quantum systems to handle superpositions of states allows them to tackle such problems in ways classical computers simply cannot.

For finance professionals and investors, the key lies in harnessing this quantum power effectively. Understanding quantum algorithms, designing quantum-ready financial models, and gaining access to quantum computing platforms will be crucial. Quantum as a Service (QaaS) platforms can be particularly useful for smaller financial institutions and individual investors looking to utilize quantum computing without the need for large upfront investment.

2. Fraud Detection and Quantum Machine Learning

Financial fraud is a constant battle for institutions and consumers alike. Quantum machine learning (QML), an amalgamation of quantum computing and artificial intelligence, can significantly enhance fraud detection by handling vast datasets and uncovering subtle patterns that might elude classical algorithms.

For those interested in implementing QML, it's crucial to understand that the transition isn't just about upgrading technology but also about upgrading skills. Teams need to be trained in the nuances of QML, and collaborations with quantum tech firms or consultants may be a fruitful avenue to explore.

3. Quantum Computing and Financial Risk Analysis

The financial industry thrives or falls on the ability to accurately predict and mitigate risk. Whether it's forecasting market trends, pricing complex derivatives, or assessing credit risk, quantum computing can provide a level of accuracy and speed that surpasses classical methodologies.

Quantum Monte Carlo simulations, for instance, can expedite complex financial modeling tasks, enabling real-time risk assessment, a capability far beyond the reach of classical computers. For risk analysts and traders, this could be a game-changer, offering a level of agility and precision that could significantly enhance decision-making processes.

4. Quantum Cryptography: The New Era of Financial Security

In a world where financial transactions are increasingly digital, security is paramount. Quantum cryptography, particularly quantum key distribution (QKD), provides unprecedented security. It harnesses the principles of quantum mechanics to share encryption keys, with any attempt at interception altering the quantum state and immediately alerting the communicators.

The challenge here is in implementing QKD systems. The financial industry, particularly banking, will need to invest in quantum-safe infrastructures. Moreover, global standards and regulations around quantum cybersecurity need to be established to ensure safe and uniform practices.

5. Quantum Computing: An Investment Horizon

Quantum computing is not just a tool for the finance industry; it's also an exciting investment avenue. Quantum tech startups are burgeoning, offering an opportunity for forward-thinking investors. However, due diligence is crucial as the quantum industry, like any emerging technology, comes with its share of risks and volatility.

As we stand on the cusp of this quantum revolution in finance, the possibilities seem limitless. However, these advances also bring new challenges – from infrastructure needs and workforce training to privacy concerns and regulatory hurdles. Tackling these effectively will require concerted effort from all stakeholders, including financial institutions, regulators, educators, and individuals.

Yet, the potential rewards – enhanced security, efficiency, and precision in financial operations – make this endeavor well worth it. As we transition into this new quantum era, we must strive not just to adapt but to shape this quantum financial landscape in a way that maximizes its benefits while minimizing its risks, ensuring a financial future that is not just more powerful but also more equitable and secure.

Private Conversations: How Quantum Secures Our Communication

In an increasingly connected world, the need for secure, private communication is more crucial than ever. Quantum mechanics, the science of the infinitesimally small, may seem an unlikely hero in this tale. Yet, it is quantum mechanics that underpins one of the most promising developments in secure communication technology: quantum cryptography. This new quantum era offers unparalleled security, fundamentally transforming our communication landscape and offering a powerful tool against cyber threats.

1. Understanding Quantum Cryptography

Quantum cryptography leverages the principles of quantum mechanics to secure data transfers, creating encrypted communication links that are virtually unbreakable. The key to this incredible security is a feature of quantum mechanics known as quantum entanglement, which allows particles to become interconnected such that the state of one instantly affects the other, no matter the distance separating them.

2. Quantum Key Distribution (QKD)

The most significant application of quantum cryptography today is Quantum Key Distribution (QKD). In QKD, cryptographic keys are transferred using quantum entangled particles. Any attempt to intercept or eavesdrop on the communication disrupts the entangled state of the particles, alerting the legitimate users to the breach.

To make the most out of QKD, users must ensure they have the necessary infrastructures in place, which includes both quantum and classical resources. This may require investment in quantum communication devices, secure communication channels, and classical computational resources.

3. Post-Quantum Cryptography

While quantum cryptography is revolutionizing secure communication, it also poses a risk to our current cryptographic systems. Most of our digital security infrastructure relies on cryptographic algorithms that could be broken by sufficiently powerful quantum computers. This has led to the development of post-quantum cryptography - cryptographic systems designed to withstand quantum computer attacks.

Understanding the quantum threat to current cryptographic systems and transitioning to post-quantum cryptographic systems is an urgent task. This requires a comprehensive audit of existing systems, a clear transition plan, and education and training for IT personnel.

4. Quantum Cryptography and Privacy

Quantum cryptography has profound implications for privacy. By providing a secure method for key distribution, it can help protect sensitive data from increasingly sophisticated cyber threats.

However, the move to quantum-secured communications also poses challenges. Privacy laws and regulations must adapt to these new technologies, and users must be educated about the potential risks and benefits of quantum-secured communications.

5. Implementing Quantum-Secure Communications

Despite the promise of quantum cryptography, implementing quantum-secure communications is a considerable challenge. It requires significant investment in new technologies and infrastructures, and there are technical hurdles to overcome, including distance limitations and the need for highly accurate alignment of quantum devices.

To implement quantum-secure communications effectively, a detailed understanding of the quantum communication landscape is crucial. A comprehensive risk assessment, considering both technical and legal aspects, will help identify the most suitable quantum cryptographic solutions. Partnerships with experienced quantum communication providers can also aid the transition, offering expert guidance and resources.

Quantum cryptography holds the potential to revolutionize secure communication, offering a level of security unachievable with classical cryptographic systems. But as with any powerful technology, it comes with its challenges and complexities. By understanding these challenges, we can navigate this new quantum landscape effectively, ensuring that our communications are not only secure but also work to uphold the privacy and freedoms we cherish. With the right approach and understanding, we can make the promise of quantum-secured communication a reality.

Smaller, Better, Brighter: Quantum Dots and the Future of Electronics

In our quest for ever-more efficient and high-performing technologies, quantum science has emerged as a game-changer, redefining the realms of possibility in numerous sectors. One such fascinating field is the development and application of quantum dots. They're minuscule, they're powerful, and they're set to revolutionize the world of electronics.

1. Quantum Dots Unveiled

Quantum dots (QDs) are nanoscale semiconductor particles, so small that they exhibit quantum mechanical properties. Depending on their size, they can emit or absorb specific frequencies of light, making them useful for a range of applications, from medicine to solar cells to next-generation display technology.

2. Quantum Dots in Display Technology

One of the most prominent applications of quantum dots today is in display technology, specifically in Quantum Dot Light Emitting Diodes (QLED) TVs. The addition of quantum dots to a regular LED display enhances color accuracy and provides a wider color spectrum, resulting in a more vibrant, lifelike picture.

But as with any technology, there are challenges. Quantum dots in their current form still require a blue LED backlight and color filters, which can limit their efficiency. Plus, there are concerns about the environmental impact of cadmium-based quantum dots. To overcome these issues, research is underway into developing cadmium-free quantum dots and new types of QD-LED displays.

3. Quantum Dots in Solar Cells

Quantum dots also have the potential to revolutionize solar power. The ability to absorb different light frequencies means QDs could significantly increase solar cell efficiency. Some researchers are exploring quantum dot-based "rainbow" solar cells, which could harvest energy across the entire solar spectrum.

But challenges remain, including the need for stable, scalable, and environmentally friendly quantum dot production. Addressing these challenges will require further research and development and potentially new manufacturing methods.

4. Quantum Dots in Medicine

Quantum dots' unique properties make them promising in various medical fields, including imaging, diagnostics, and targeted drug delivery. For example, their high luminescence can improve contrast in medical imaging, and their size-tunable properties can be used to design precise diagnostic tools or drug delivery systems.

However, concerns about toxicity and biocompatibility need to be addressed before QD-based medical technologies can become commonplace. Continued research and rigorous testing will be essential to realizing the potential of quantum dots in medicine.

5. Navigating the Quantum Dot Landscape

The potential of quantum dots is exciting, but successfully navigating the QD landscape requires an understanding of both the opportunities and challenges involved. Research and development are needed to address issues like toxicity and environmental impact, and new manufacturing and handling processes may need to be developed.

Engaging with quantum dot technology also means staying informed about the latest research developments and understanding the potential risks and benefits. Involving quantum experts early in the process and investing in quantum literacy can pay dividends in successfully navigating the quantum dot landscape.

Quantum dots, in their brilliance and potential, are emblematic of the quantum revolution that's reshaping our world. With their promise for improved displays, more efficient solar cells, and groundbreaking medical technologies, they represent the thrilling confluence of nanotechnology and quantum physics.

By recognizing their potential and addressing the challenges head-on, we can ensure that we harness the power of quantum dots to its fullest, propelling our electronics into the quantum age.

Chapter 5: Quantum Technologies and National Security

Quantum Cryptography: Redefining Cybersecurity

As we sail into the quantum age, an era where the fundamental principles of physics are harnessed to create unprecedented technologies, we must also brace ourselves for the impending wave of transformation it will bring to our security landscape. Quantum technologies promise to redefine the way we approach cybersecurity, leading the charge is quantum cryptography. Here, we delve into what quantum cryptography is, why it is important, and how it could redefine cybersecurity and national security.

1. Quantum Cryptography Explained

Quantum cryptography, also known as quantum key distribution (QKD), is a method that uses the principles of quantum mechanics to encrypt and decrypt data. It takes advantage of the unique behavior of photons to transmit secure data over a distance. If an eavesdropper tries to intercept the data, the act of measuring the quantum state of the photons will change their state, alerting the sender and receiver to the presence of an intruder.

2. The Potential of Quantum Cryptography

The potential applications of quantum cryptography are vast. It could be used to secure financial transactions, to protect sensitive government information, or to safeguard critical infrastructure like power grids and water systems. In particular, quantum cryptography could play a crucial role in national security. As countries around the world invest in developing quantum technologies, there is a growing recognition that quantum cryptography could be a game-changer for secure communication. The ability to detect eavesdropping attempts could help prevent cyber attacks and protect national secrets.

3. The Challenges Ahead

However, like any emerging technology, quantum cryptography is not without its challenges. Firstly, the technology required for QKD is complex and expensive. Creating a practical, scalable, and affordable system that can be widely deployed is still a work in progress. Secondly, QKD requires a direct line of sight between sender and receiver, which makes it difficult to use over long distances or through obstacles.

Addressing these issues will require significant investment in research and development, and the solutions will likely come from a combination of advancements in technology, policy, and standards.

4. The Quantum Arms Race

The development of quantum technologies, including quantum cryptography, has led to what some are calling a "quantum arms race." Countries like the U.S., China, Canada, and several European nations are investing heavily in quantum research, eager to be at the forefront of the quantum revolution.

While competition can drive innovation, it can also lead to challenges, especially in the realm of national security. Balancing the pursuit of technological superiority with the need for cooperation and collaboration to establish global standards will be a delicate task.

5. Preparing for the Quantum Future

To prepare for the quantum future, governments, businesses, and individuals alike will need to stay informed about the latest advancements in quantum technology. This includes understanding the potential benefits and risks associated with quantum cryptography and other quantum technologies.

In addition, fostering a strong quantum workforce will be essential. This means investing in quantum education and training to ensure we have the skilled professionals needed to drive the quantum revolution forward.

Quantum cryptography holds the promise to revolutionize cybersecurity and transform the landscape of national security. As we continue to navigate the uncharted waters of the quantum age, it is crucial that we remain vigilant, adaptive, and prepared to embrace the changes and challenges that come our way. By doing so, we can harness the power of quantum technology to create a safer, more secure world.

Quantum Espionage: A New Era of Stealth and Information Gathering

In the shadowy realm of spycraft and counterintelligence, the rules of the game are always shifting. As quantum technologies continue to evolve, they are ushering in a new era of stealth and information gathering. Quantum espionage, as it is becoming known, promises to redefine traditional notions of spying, bringing with it a host of new opportunities and challenges.

1. What is Quantum Espionage?

Quantum espionage refers to the use of quantum technologies in spying and intelligence-gathering operations. This can involve a range of applications, from using quantum encryption to protect communications to harnessing quantum computers to break traditional encryption methods. The idea is to leverage the unique properties of quantum physics - such as superposition and entanglement - to gain an edge in the world of intelligence and counterintelligence.

2. The Opportunities

Quantum espionage presents several exciting opportunities. For one, quantum technologies can provide an unprecedented level of security for communications.

Quantum key distribution (QKD), for example, allows for the creation of encryption keys that are virtually unbreakable, ensuring that sensitive information can be transmitted securely.

Furthermore, quantum technologies could give rise to new methods of surveillance. Theoretically, a quantum radar could detect objects with far greater sensitivity than traditional radar, enabling it to pick up stealth aircraft or submarines that would otherwise remain undetected. Quantum sensors could also be employed in a variety of surveillance applications, offering enhanced capabilities in areas like facial recognition or signal detection.

3. The Challenges

But along with these opportunities come significant challenges. Quantum computers, for instance, have the potential to render traditional encryption methods obsolete. This presents a serious threat to national security, as it could allow adversaries to break encryption and gain access to sensitive information.

Moreover, the very nature of quantum technologies - with their reliance on delicate quantum states that can be easily disturbed - presents practical challenges in terms of development and deployment. Quantum devices are highly sensitive to environmental factors and require stringent operating conditions, making them difficult to implement in real-world settings.

4. Navigating the Quantum Espionage Landscape

So, how can nations navigate this emerging landscape of quantum espionage? There are several strategies that could be employed.

First, investment in research and development is critical. Developing robust quantum technologies and understanding their potential applications in the realm of espionage will be key to staying ahead of the curve.

Second, nations will need to prioritize quantum education and training. Cultivating a workforce skilled in quantum technologies will be crucial in driving innovation and ensuring national security.

Third, countries will need to develop quantum-resistant encryption methods. As quantum computers advance, so too must our encryption techniques to ensure that sensitive information remains secure.

5. The Role of Collaboration and Regulation

Lastly, collaboration and regulation will play a critical role in shaping the quantum espionage landscape. Nations will need to work together to develop standards and policies for the use of quantum technologies in espionage. This could involve international agreements on acceptable use, as well as cooperation in research and development.

At the same time, regulation will be important to ensure that the use of quantum technologies in espionage is conducted ethically and responsibly. This could include laws and guidelines on the use of quantum technologies in surveillance, as well as safeguards to protect against their misuse.

The era of quantum espionage is upon us, bringing with it a host of new possibilities and challenges. As nations navigate this uncharted territory, they will need to balance the pursuit of technological advancement with the need for security, collaboration, and ethical responsibility. By doing so, they can harness the power of quantum technologies to redefine espionage, while ensuring that the game of spycraft continues to be played on a level field.

The Role of Quantum Computers in Encryption

Quantum computers, due to their unique processing capabilities, have opened up a Pandora's box in the realm of information security. They present both an unprecedented opportunity for creating ultra-secure systems and a grave threat to the existing security infrastructure. This dual role has precipitated a reevaluation of classical encryption methodologies and brought quantum encryption into focus.

1. Quantum Computing: A Brief Overview
To appreciate the influence of quantum computers in the realm of encryption, it's crucial to understand their fundamental difference from classical computers. Classical

computers encode information in binary digits, or bits, each of which can represent either a 0 or 1. Quantum computers, on the other hand, use quantum bits or "qubits", that can exist in multiple states at once, thanks to the principle of superposition. Qubits can be both 0 and 1 simultaneously, leading to a vast increase in processing power.

2. The Threat to Classical Encryption

One of the most significant challenges that quantum computers pose is to the realm of classical encryption. Many contemporary encryption algorithms rely on the difficulty of factoring large prime numbers—a problem that classical computers can't solve in a reasonable time. RSA encryption, for example, is based on this principle.

Quantum computers, with their exponential processing capabilities, are expected to readily solve these problems, thus threatening to dismantle the current security architecture. Shor's algorithm, a quantum algorithm, can factorize large prime numbers efficiently, spelling doom for RSA and similar encryption protocols.

3. The Opportunity: Quantum Encryption

While quantum computers threaten classical encryption, they also present an opportunity for creating ultra-secure encryption systems using the principles of quantum mechanics. Quantum Key Distribution (QKD) is a prime example of this opportunity. It uses the principle of quantum entanglement to create a pair of entangled qubits that mirror each other's state no matter the distance between them.

This property is used to create a shared secret key between two parties, providing security in two ways. First, any attempt at eavesdropping disturbs the entangled state of the qubits, alerting the communicating parties to the intrusion. Second, thanks to the 'no-cloning theorem' of quantum mechanics, an eavesdropper cannot duplicate the qubits, making it impossible for them to acquire the key without detection.

4. The Transition: Post-Quantum Cryptography

As the threat of quantum computers becomes increasingly apparent, the shift towards 'post-quantum cryptography' has gathered pace. These are cryptographic algorithms designed to be secure even in the presence of powerful quantum computers. Many of these algorithms are based on mathematical problems that are believed to be resistant to quantum computing attacks.

Lattice-based cryptography, for example, is one promising area in this field. It relies on the difficulty of finding the shortest vector in a high-dimensional lattice—a problem which is believed to be hard for both classical and quantum computers.

5. Policy, Cooperation, and the Way Forward

As we move into the quantum era, cooperation and policy-making will play crucial roles. International collaboration is essential for setting standards for quantum encryption and post-quantum cryptography to avoid creating a disorganized, disjointed security landscape.

Organizations like the National Institute of Standards and Technology (NIST) in the United States are already working towards setting these standards by testing and vetting post-quantum cryptographic algorithms. Similarly, the ETSI (European Telecommunications Standards Institute) has been active in the standardization of QKD.

The advent of quantum computers is a paradigm shift that threatens to undermine classical encryption while simultaneously paving the way for quantum encryption. The balance of this dual impact will be determined by how swiftly and efficiently we adapt to this change, developing quantum-resistant algorithms and setting global standards for quantum-based encryption systems. The role of quantum computers in encryption, therefore, is not just disruptive but also constructive, setting the stage for the next chapter in secure communications.

International Relations in the Quantum Age: Balance of Power and Quantum Diplomacy

In this era of swift and groundbreaking technological progress, international relations are increasingly influenced by the interplay of new technologies. Quantum technology, with its potential to revolutionize various sectors, from computing and cryptography to sensors and imaging, is no exception. This chapter seeks to examine the implications of quantum technology on the international balance of power and the emerging concept of quantum diplomacy.

1. Quantum Technology: A Paradigm Shift

Quantum technology harnesses the principles of quantum mechanics to enable unprecedented capabilities, such as superposition and entanglement, resulting in quantum computers' computational power dwarfing that of the most powerful classical supercomputers. This technological revolution extends beyond just raw computational power, with implications for data security, material science, healthcare, and more.

2. Balance of Power: A Quantum Perspective

In international relations, balance of power refers to a state of stability between competing forces or nations. As quantum technology advances, it has the potential to disrupt this balance. Quantum supremacy, the point at which quantum computers outperform classical ones, can give a significant edge to the nation that achieves it first.

Quantum technologies can provide strategic advantages in military affairs, economy, communications, and information security. Quantum sensors could improve the precision of surveillance and navigation systems, and quantum computers could solve complex optimization problems in logistics and planning or break cryptographic systems, fundamentally altering the nature of warfare and intelligence.

3. Quantum Diplomacy: Emerging Strategies

Quantum diplomacy refers to international relations strategies that involve cooperation and negotiation around quantum technologies. The objective is to manage the challenges and exploit the opportunities presented by quantum science.

One key aspect of quantum diplomacy is managing the race for quantum supremacy. Unchecked competition could lead to an unstable, high-stakes "quantum arms race." Quantum diplomacy seeks to manage this competition and encourage international cooperation.

4. Collaborations and Partnerships

Encouraging international collaborations and partnerships in quantum research could foster a cooperative rather than competitive environment. Multilateral agreements can help set shared standards for the development and use of quantum technologies, promoting their safe and equitable use. This may take the form of joint research projects, shared quantum infrastructure, or student and scientist exchange programs.

5. Quantum Ethics and Governance

Quantum diplomacy must also address ethical and governance issues. This includes questions of data security and privacy in the age of quantum computing and the ethical use of quantum technologies in areas like healthcare and AI. International bodies may need to formulate and adopt quantum-specific agreements or codes of conduct.

6. Navigating the Quantum Future

The path to navigating international relations in the quantum age is fraught with challenges. However, these challenges can be addressed through proactive diplomacy, fostering international cooperation, and creating a shared vision for the quantum future. It involves not just politicians and diplomats, but scientists, ethicists, and technologists.

The future of international relations in the quantum age depends on our ability to balance competition with cooperation, leveraging the power of quantum technologies while mitigating their risks. The quantum age offers a unique opportunity to reshape international relations and foster a more cooperative, inclusive global community.

Quantum technologies are set to redefine the future, including the balance of power among nations. However, the concept of quantum diplomacy provides a pathway to navigate these changes. By fostering international cooperation, setting global standards, and addressing ethical and governance issues, we can harness the power of quantum technologies to create a more secure and equitable future.

Quantum Transport: Securing Global Commerce and Trade

As the realms of quantum technology and global commerce converge, an intriguing question arises: How might quantum innovations bolster the security and efficiency of worldwide trade and transportation? In this section, we will examine the substantial implications of quantum technology for global commerce, focusing particularly on how it can fortify transport systems and secure economic exchanges.

1. Understanding Quantum Transport

To understand how quantum mechanics can transform global commerce and trade, one must first grasp what quantum transport is. In essence, quantum transport deals with the flow of quantum information or particles from one location to another, following the principles of quantum mechanics. From this perspective, we can look at two aspects: quantum communication and quantum navigation.

2. Quantum Communication: Building Trust in Global Commerce

Secure communication is the backbone of international commerce. Buyers and sellers, often located in different parts of the world, must communicate to negotiate deals, share sensitive financial information, and coordinate logistics. Quantum technologies offer an unparalleled level of security in these communications, fortifying trust between trading partners.

Quantum key distribution (QKD) is one such innovation. In QKD, cryptographic keys are distributed using quantum states, which are sensitive to any form of eavesdropping. If an unauthorized third party tries to intercept the communication, the quantum state will change, alerting the legitimate users of the interference.

3. Quantum Navigation: Ensuring Accurate and Secure Logistics

When it comes to transporting goods around the globe, accuracy and security are of utmost importance. Quantum navigation, using high-precision quantum sensors, can significantly enhance both.

Quantum sensors exploit the principles of quantum superposition and entanglement to make ultra-precise measurements. Quantum accelerometers and gyroscopes, for example, can provide exact positional information, improving the accuracy of navigation systems, reducing logistic errors, and enhancing operational efficiency.

4. Overcoming Challenges

While the applications of quantum technology in global commerce and transport promise transformative benefits, they also come with a unique set of challenges.

Firstly, quantum technologies are still in their infancy, and much work needs to be done to mature and scale them. Secondly, they require substantial investment in infrastructure and workforce training. Lastly, they can also introduce new security threats. For instance, while quantum computers can enhance security through QKD, they also have the potential to break current encryption algorithms.

5. The Path Forward: Quantum Readiness

To leverage quantum technologies' full potential in global commerce and transport, organizations need to develop "quantum readiness." This encompasses understanding the potentials and pitfalls of quantum technology, investing in research and development, and upskilling the workforce.

Moreover, international cooperation and legislation are crucial. Governments, academic institutions, and private companies should collaborate to develop shared standards and regulations for the deployment and use of quantum technologies in global commerce and transport.

The advent of quantum technologies brings a new dawn for global commerce and transport, offering enhanced communication security and navigation precision. But like every sunrise, it casts long shadows—of technical challenges, infrastructural needs, and security risks. As we stride into this brave new quantum world, our task is to harness the sunlight while acknowledging and addressing the shadows.

Chapter 6: Emerging Trends in Quantum Technology

Quantum Sensor Applications: From Environment Monitoring to Healthcare

In the bustling domain of quantum technology, one of the most promising developments that has emerged in recent years is the quantum sensor. These devices, capable of detecting and responding to quantum interactions, have shown immense potential to revolutionize diverse fields, from environmental monitoring to healthcare and beyond. A quantum sensor operates based on the fundamental principles of quantum mechanics—superposition and entanglement. The delicate nature of quantum states allows these sensors to detect changes in the environment with unprecedented precision and sensitivity.

In the realm of environmental monitoring, for instance, these sensors can offer precise measurements of various environmental parameters like temperature, humidity, pressure, and magnetic fields. Such high-precision data acquisition can facilitate more accurate climate modelling, more effective pollution control, and more informed policy-making. In a world grappling with environmental challenges, the importance of such advancements cannot be overstated.

Quantum sensors also hold immense potential in healthcare. Imagine a world where doctors can detect diseases like cancer at the earliest stages, or even before they develop, significantly improving patient outcomes. Quantum sensors can make this possible. They can detect minuscule changes in the human body that indicate disease, even at the molecular level. For example, changes in cellular environments, like temperature or pH, can indicate the onset of a disease.

Moreover, in neuroscience, quantum sensors could allow us to map brain activity with unparalleled precision, providing insights into neurological disorders and paving the way for novel treatments. In drug discovery, quantum sensors can be used to study the interaction of potential drug molecules with their target receptors at an atomic level, leading to more effective and safer medicines.

However, these advances do not come without challenges. Quantum sensors, like other quantum technologies, are highly sensitive to their environments. Even slight disturbances can disrupt their operation, leading to errors. The field must therefore devise ways to protect these sensors from environmental noise. Moreover, the deployment of quantum sensors on a large scale will require significant advances in engineering and manufacturing, along with robust legal and ethical guidelines to ensure their safe and responsible use.

So, what does the path forward look like? The journey to harnessing the full potential of quantum sensors is a marathon, not a sprint. It requires continued investment in quantum research and development, fostering collaborations between physicists, engineers, medical professionals, environmental scientists, policy makers, and others.

Moreover, it also requires nurturing a quantum-ready workforce. Education and training programs in quantum science and technologies must be expanded and made accessible to diverse audiences. Such efforts can ensure that the benefits of quantum sensors are reaped across sectors, from climate science to healthcare.

Quantum sensors represent a new frontier in the quantum revolution, offering a tantalizing glimpse of what the quantum future might hold. As we continue to explore and expand this frontier, we can look forward to a world where quantum sensors play a crucial role in safeguarding our environment and enhancing our health. It's a journey of discovery, and like all journeys, it promises to be as exciting as the destination itself.

Revolutionary Quantum Technology: Quantum Computers to Quantum Internet

The world is standing on the precipice of a technological revolution, an era promising transformative changes across all sectors of society. Quantum technology, the lynchpin of this imminent revolution, is changing the face of how we compute, communicate, and comprehend the world around us. Quantum computers and the quantum internet are two prominent representatives of this futuristic technology that are set to rewrite the rules of digital evolution.

Diving into the world of quantum computers, we uncover a fundamentally new paradigm of computing. Classical computers, the workhorses of today's digital world, work on bits, the smallest unit of data, that can exist in one of two states: 0 or 1. However, quantum computers operate on quantum bits, or qubits. These qubits can exist not just in a state of 0 or 1, but in a superposition of states, which essentially means they can be 0, 1, or both at the same time.

This superposition of states, along with the phenomenon of quantum entanglement, where qubits become intertwined and the state of one qubit instantaneously influences the state of the other, regardless of the distance separating them, paves the way for quantum computers to process massive amounts of data and solve complex problems far more swiftly than their classical counterparts.

Imagine a world where complex problems in fields such as cryptography, material science, drug discovery, climate modeling, and many more, which would take classical computers years or even centuries to solve, could be unraveled by quantum computers in mere seconds or minutes. Such is the promising potential of quantum computing.

However, with this potential comes a fair share of challenges that need overcoming. One of the major hurdles is the issue of qubit stability, or coherence time. Quantum states are extremely delicate and can be easily disturbed by their environment, a process known as decoherence. Scientists across the globe are tirelessly working on developing innovative techniques to stabilize qubits and prolong their coherence times.

Beyond quantum computing, another quantum marvel that's making waves is the quantum internet. This isn't just a faster or more secure version of the existing internet, but a completely new network, where information is sent and received in a fundamentally different way. The quantum internet will leverage the power of quantum mechanics, specifically quantum entanglement, to transmit information securely and instantaneously.

In a quantum internet, data is transmitted using quantum states of light particles, or photons. These photons can be entangled, such that any change to one will immediately affect its partner, regardless of the distance separating them, allowing for communication that is not only instantaneous but also highly secure.

However, just as with quantum computing, building a quantum internet presents unique challenges. Storing and transmitting quantum information while preventing it from being lost or altered is no easy task. Moreover, the development of a new quantum network infrastructure necessitates the collaboration of network engineers, quantum physicists, computer scientists, and industry leaders. Despite these challenges, progress is being made, and pilot quantum networks have already been developed in several countries.

Solving these challenges and fully harnessing the potential of quantum technologies will require a multi-pronged approach. On one front, continued investment in research and development is needed to push the boundaries of what's possible in quantum computing and quantum networking. On another front, public and private sectors must collaborate to build a robust quantum infrastructure, from quantum hardware to quantum algorithms and applications.

Further, as quantum technologies become increasingly integrated into our society, questions of ethics, policy, and regulation will take center stage. We must ensure that these technologies are used responsibly and that their benefits are accessible to all. Creating legal frameworks and ethical guidelines that account for the unique characteristics of quantum technologies is therefore paramount.

Education and workforce training is another critical piece of the puzzle. The quantum revolution will demand a new breed of professionals fluent in the language of quantum mechanics. Encouraging the growth of quantum education and fostering a quantum-ready workforce will be key to realizing the full potential of quantum technologies.

As we stand at the cusp of the quantum era, it's exciting to imagine a world reshaped by quantum computers and the quantum internet. From groundbreaking scientific discoveries to a new level of digital security, the quantum revolution promises a future brimming with possibilities. It's a journey that demands collective effort, foresight, and commitment, and like all revolutions, it promises to be transformative, disruptive, and inevitably, extraordinary.

Quantum Technology Progress: What the Future Holds

The quantum leap is not just a figurative expression anymore. Quantum technology, a field that leverages the bizarre and yet fascinating rules of quantum mechanics, is beginning to shape a promising future. To understand what lies ahead, we must appreciate the enormous strides quantum technology has made in recent years, the challenges it faces, and the roadmap for the coming years. In doing so, we hope to provide answers and solutions to the potential hurdles you, as a reader and possible contributor to the field, may encounter.

To begin with, quantum computing, one of the most recognized aspects of quantum technology, has made significant progress in the last decade. Quantum computers operate on the principles of superposition and entanglement, enabling them to handle a tremendous amount of data and perform complex calculations at a speed that is beyond the capabilities of classical computers. Companies like IBM, Google, and Microsoft are heavily invested in developing scalable quantum computers, and breakthroughs are announced frequently. Despite the impressive advancements, the path to achieving 'Quantum Supremacy' - where quantum computers can perform tasks inconceivable by classical computers - is laden with significant challenges.

Decoherence and error correction pose notable obstacles. The delicate quantum states need to be isolated from all forms of external interference, and even then, they last only for a brief period. Additionally, quantum computations are vulnerable to errors, and developing robust quantum error correction methods is a pressing need. As a prospective researcher or entrepreneur in quantum technology, working on these challenges would be of immense value to the field.

Quantum communication is another promising area that holds potential to revolutionize the way we share and secure information. Quantum Key Distribution (QKD), a method that uses quantum states to encode and transmit keys for encrypted communication, offers theoretically unbreakable security. The world has already seen the successful implementation of QKD in commercial settings, with more advancements on the horizon. However, realizing a full-fledged quantum internet that allows quantum communication over long distances is still a challenge due to the difficulty in preserving entanglement over extended lengths.

Emerging trends also indicate the advent of quantum sensing, capable of measuring physical quantities with unprecedented precision. Quantum sensors could bring dramatic improvements in various fields, from healthcare to navigation, climate science to materials science. Yet, quantum sensors share the common challenge with other quantum technologies, requiring extremely stable and controlled environments.

Looking into the future of quantum technology, we can expect an array of advancements. First, expect quantum computers to grow more robust and powerful, inching closer to achieving Quantum Supremacy. Companies and researchers around the globe are already experimenting with 'Quantum Advantage', where quantum computers outperform classical computers for specific tasks. As we overcome hurdles like decoherence and quantum error correction, we might witness the rise of quantum computers that can tackle problems currently out of our reach.

The development of a quantum internet is another major milestone we are likely to achieve. While we already have small-scale quantum networks, the establishment of global quantum networks will be a game-changer. It will not only revolutionize secure communication but also allow distributed quantum computing and quantum-enhanced measurements.

Next, we are likely to see quantum sensors become more commonplace, integrated into various sectors of the economy. With enhanced sensitivity and precision, they will significantly improve diagnostic capabilities, environmental monitoring, and even our understanding of quantum physics.

While these developments are promising, the journey towards a quantum future is not just about technological advancements. Equally important are the considerations of quantum policy, ethics, education, and inclusion.

As a society, we must ensure that quantum technologies are developed and deployed responsibly and that their benefits are accessible to all. This will require careful crafting of policy and legal frameworks, fostering quantum literacy, and promoting diversity and inclusion in the quantum workforce.

Finally, there's a crucial role for international cooperation in the future of quantum technology. Quantum advancements are not confined within national borders. Collaborative efforts in research, shared standards, and policy alignment will be necessary to prevent a quantum divide and to tackle global challenges collectively.

The future of quantum technology is bright, brimming with potential, and full of opportunities for those willing to dive into its depths.

As we navigate through this exciting journey, the goal should not just be about conquering challenges but also about shaping a quantum future that benefits all of humanity.

Whether you are a researcher, an entrepreneur, a policy-maker, or just an intrigued reader, you can contribute to this shared vision. After all, the quantum leap is ours to make.

Chapter 7: Building the Quantum Workforce

The Future Job Market: Quantum Skills in Demand

As quantum technologies gain momentum, they're not just shaping the future of computation, communication, and sensing – they're also shaping the future of work. Quantum technologies are on the verge of becoming mainstream, and this change brings a transformative shift in the job market. There's a growing demand for quantum-literate professionals, and this shift will only amplify in the future. If you're wondering how to navigate this landscape and be part of the quantum workforce, you're in the right place.

To understand this shift, let's first consider the sectors impacted by quantum technologies. Quantum computing has the potential to revolutionize industries like pharmaceuticals, logistics, finance, and artificial intelligence, which rely heavily on computational prowess. Quantum communication and quantum cryptography can significantly enhance the cybersecurity domain, providing impregnable security protocols. Quantum sensing, with its high precision, has applications in fields as diverse as healthcare, environmental monitoring, navigation, and defense.

The growing influence of quantum technology translates into an increasing need for quantum-skilled professionals. However, it's not just about researchers and developers. The quantum ecosystem is broad, involving roles like engineers, technicians, educators, policy makers, ethical consultants, and business leaders.

Given this scenario, what are the skills that will be in demand in the quantum job market? Here's a list to start with:

1. **Quantum Information Science:** This involves understanding quantum mechanics, quantum computing algorithms, quantum error correction, and more. This skill set will be crucial for those involved in research, development, and application of quantum technologies.

2. **Quantum Engineering:** Building quantum systems involves not only quantum principles but also skills like electrical engineering, cryogenics, and material science.

3. **Quantum Programming:** With quantum computers becoming more accessible, the ability to code quantum algorithms using quantum programming languages like Qiskit, Cirq, and Q# is becoming increasingly relevant.

4. **Data Science and AI:** Quantum computers will be used to process vast amounts of data and accelerate machine learning. As such, skills in data science and AI will be valuable in the quantum landscape.

5. **Cybersecurity:** Understanding quantum cryptography and post-quantum cryptography will be important in the quantum-enhanced cybersecurity landscape.

6. **Policy, Ethics, and Legal knowledge:** As quantum technologies get integrated into society, we need professionals who understand their societal, ethical, and legal implications. This is crucial in areas like data privacy, standard-setting, international cooperation, and more.

7. **Business Acumen:** Like any other field, quantum technology needs leaders who understand its commercial and strategic aspects. This includes areas like quantum project management, strategic decision-making, market analysis, and so forth.

8. **Communication and Education:** Communicating quantum concepts effectively, to diverse audiences, is crucial. This includes educators who can foster quantum literacy, and communicators who can facilitate dialogue between different stakeholders.

Given these skills in demand, how can you, as a prospective quantum professional, prepare for this future job market? Here are some strategies:

Education and Training: Begin by acquiring a solid foundation in quantum mechanics and quantum information science. Universities worldwide are offering quantum-related courses, both at the undergraduate and postgraduate levels. For those who prefer flexible learning, numerous online platforms provide quantum computing courses.

Interdisciplinary Approach: Quantum technology is inherently interdisciplinary. Whether you're an engineer, a computer scientist, a physicist, or even a social scientist, you can find a role in the quantum ecosystem. Consider supplementing your primary skill set with knowledge in complementary areas.

Practical Experience: Try to gain hands-on experience with quantum systems. This could involve using cloud-based quantum computing platforms, participating in quantum coding competitions, or interning at quantum technology companies.

Stay Current: Quantum technology is evolving rapidly. Stay updated with the latest advancements, either by following quantum-focused blogs, attending conferences and webinars, or participating in quantum technology forums.

Network: Join the quantum community. Attend meetups, participate in online communities, connect with peers and experts in the field. This can provide valuable insights, mentorship, and even job opportunities.

The transition to a quantum future may seem daunting, but it's also filled with opportunities. As the landscape evolves, new roles will emerge, and existing roles will transform. Navigating this change is not about predicting the future perfectly – it's about staying agile, staying curious, and continually learning. So whether you're a student considering a career in quantum technology, a professional contemplating a shift, or an educator wondering how to equip your students for a quantum future, remember this: the quantum wave is here, and it's ours to ride.

Educating the Quantum Pioneers: Shaping Tomorrow's Workforce

The rise of quantum technologies brings an essential task to the forefront - preparing the next generation of innovators, the quantum pioneers. Education systems worldwide are now facing the challenge of how to shape a quantum-literate workforce effectively. It's a complex task given the multidisciplinary, abstract, and rapidly-evolving nature of quantum technology. However, the rewards are also immense, from advancing technology to solving societal challenges. In this section, we'll delve into strategies that educators, policy-makers, and learners can adopt to shape and navigate this new quantum education landscape.

One of the first challenges in educating quantum pioneers is the abstract nature of quantum mechanics. The principles of superposition and entanglement, the cornerstones of quantum technology, can seem counterintuitive, even bizarre, compared to the classical physics we're familiar with. Hence, it's crucial to develop educational approaches that make these concepts accessible and relatable.

One such approach is the use of interactive visualizations and simulations. For example, quantum computing simulators allow learners to visualize quantum states, execute quantum algorithms, and see their results, providing an intuitive understanding of quantum phenomena. Likewise, augmented reality (AR) and virtual reality (VR) tools can enable learners to "experience" quantum phenomena, making abstract concepts tangible. Another strategy is to weave quantum concepts into the broader science curriculum. Quantum mechanics shouldn't just be an advanced topic for university-level physics students - elements of it can be integrated earlier. For instance, high school physics could introduce the concept of light as both a particle and a wave, a fundamental quantum idea.

Another critical aspect of quantum education is fostering an interdisciplinary mindset. Quantum technology is not just about physics - it intertwines with fields like computer science, engineering, mathematics, and even philosophy and ethics. Educators can encourage this interdisciplinary thinking by designing courses that highlight these connections. For example, a quantum computing course could incorporate aspects of linear algebra (from mathematics), algorithm design (from computer science), and quantum mechanics (from physics).

Alongside the hard skills in quantum technologies, we also need to cultivate the complementary 'soft' skills. These include critical thinking, to understand and navigate the complexities of quantum technologies; creativity, to innovate and solve problems; and communication skills, to explain quantum concepts to different audiences, from peers to policymakers to the public. These skills are invaluable not just in quantum technologies, but in any career path.

A significant shift in quantum education is the use of online learning platforms. They provide flexibility, allowing learners to explore quantum concepts at their own pace, and also broaden access, reaching students who may not have quantum courses in their local institutions. Massive Open Online Courses (MOOCs) on quantum computing are now available from various universities and companies. There are also interactive online textbooks, like the Quantum Country mnemonic medium by Michael Nielsen and Andy Matuschak, which leverages spaced repetition to enhance learning.

In addition to individual learners, these online resources are also valuable for educators, who themselves may be learning about quantum technologies. They provide a readily available source of material, which educators can use to develop their quantum courses or workshops.

The role of industry in quantum education is another emerging trend. Many quantum technology companies are investing in education, from offering internships and scholarships to organizing coding contests and summer schools. They're not just doing this out of altruism - they have a vested interest in developing a quantum-skilled workforce, which they'll need as they grow.

However, while these industry-led initiatives are beneficial, we should also be mindful of potential issues. For instance, if a company's quantum platform or language becomes the default teaching tool, it could limit the learners' perspective and skills to that particular platform. As such, it's important to maintain a balance and diversity in the quantum education landscape.

Lastly, it's important to consider equity in quantum education. The benefits of quantum technologies should not be confined to a privileged few - they should be accessible to all. This involves addressing barriers like geographical disparities, underrepresentation of certain groups in STEM, and the digital divide. Initiatives like scholarships for underrepresented groups, mentorship programs, and efforts to localize online courses can help make quantum education more inclusive.

While educating the quantum pioneers presents challenges, it also offers exciting opportunities to rethink how we teach and learn science. It's a collaborative endeavor, involving educators, learners, policy-makers, and industry. It's also an ongoing process, requiring us to adapt and learn as quantum technologies evolve. However, the goal is clear - to empower the next generation with the skills and curiosity to explore the quantum world and leverage its potential to shape our collective future.

Leading the Quantum Shift: New Requirements for Leaders

As we stand on the precipice of the quantum revolution, the business landscape is shifting rapidly. A transformation is looming that promises to redefine how we process information, communicate, and solve complex problems. Naturally, this presents both opportunities and challenges for leaders across sectors. The question becomes: how can leaders effectively guide their organizations through this quantum shift? What new skills, mindsets, and strategies are needed? In this section, we'll delve into these new requirements for leaders.

At the heart of the quantum revolution is an inherent complexity, stemming from the principles of quantum mechanics that challenge our everyday intuition. For leaders, this means that the first requirement is an understanding – not necessarily a deep technical knowledge, but a fundamental grasp of what quantum technologies are, what they can do, and what they cannot do. This understanding is crucial for making informed decisions about investing in quantum technologies, assessing their potential impact, and communicating effectively about them.

Bridging the knowledge gap doesn't have to be a solo journey. Leaders can leverage their teams, fostering a learning culture that encourages curiosity, exploration, and sharing of knowledge. They can also seek collaborations with academia or industry partners, gaining insights from their expertise. Resources such as online courses, webinars, and whitepapers can help leaders develop their quantum literacy.

Another vital requirement for leaders in the quantum shift is foresight. Quantum technologies are not just about the future – they're about multiple potential futures. What will quantum computers be capable of in five, ten, or twenty years? How will quantum communication change our information infrastructure? How will quantum sensors transform industries from healthcare to aerospace?

Given these uncertainties, leaders need to adopt strategic foresight, exploring these different futures, assessing their implications, and preparing for them. This could involve scenario planning exercises, trend analysis, or consulting with futurists and experts. It also involves cultivating an adaptive mindset, being ready to adjust strategies as the quantum landscape evolves.

In the quantum shift, collaboration is more than a nice-to-have – it's a necessity. Quantum technology development requires interdisciplinary teams, combining expertise from physics, computer science, engineering, and more. Leaders, therefore, need to foster a collaborative culture, encouraging cross-disciplinary communication and learning. They also need to build and manage partnerships, be it with other companies for joint ventures, with academia for research, or with government for policy advocacy.

One of the distinct challenges in leading the quantum shift is the ethical and societal implications of quantum technologies. From data privacy in quantum communication to algorithmic fairness in quantum machine learning, leaders need to navigate these complex issues. This requires an understanding of the ethical aspects, engaging with stakeholders, and developing ethical guidelines or principles for their organization. It's about leading with responsibility and integrity, ensuring that the quantum shift benefits society at large and doesn't exacerbate existing inequalities.

Risk management is another crucial skill for leaders in the quantum shift. While quantum technologies offer immense potential, they also present risks. For instance, quantum computing could disrupt current encryption systems, posing cybersecurity risks. Quantum systems also have unique vulnerabilities, like the need for ultra-cold environments or the sensitivity to external disturbances.

Leaders need to understand these risks, assess their potential impact, and develop mitigation strategies. This could involve investing in quantum-safe encryption methods, implementing robust cybersecurity practices, or designing fault-tolerant quantum systems. Risk management in the quantum shift also means embracing uncertainty and learning from failures, viewing them as opportunities for learning and improvement.

Finally, leading the quantum shift requires an innovative mindset. Quantum technologies are redefining what's possible, opening up new avenues for innovation. Leaders need to cultivate this innovative thinking, encouraging their teams to explore new ideas, question assumptions, and challenge the status quo. It's about creating an environment where creativity thrives, where ideas are shared and nurtured, and where innovation is recognized and rewarded.

Leading the quantum shift presents a unique set of requirements – from understanding and foresight to collaboration, ethical leadership, risk management, and innovation. These are not just skills to be learned, but mindsets to be cultivated. The quantum shift is not a destination but a journey of continuous learning, adaptation, and growth. By embracing these new requirements, leaders can navigate this quantum shift effectively, steering their organizations towards a future where quantum technologies unlock new possibilities and deliver value to all stakeholders.

The Quantum Job Hunt: Mapping Out Your Future Career

As the quantum revolution takes shape, new career opportunities are cropping up, with industries spanning from technology to healthcare, finance to aerospace, and more, seeking quantum-savvy professionals. In this section, we're going to map out your future career, exploring key steps and strategies to break into the quantum field, and how to navigate the quantum job hunt effectively.

First and foremost, understanding the quantum landscape is pivotal. What roles are available? Which industries are adopting quantum technologies? What skills are in demand? Familiarize yourself with the quantum ecosystem – the key players, the cutting-edge developments, and the trends shaping the field. Make use of resources like industry reports, job listings, company websites, and social media to gain insights into the quantum job market.

Once you have a handle on the landscape, the next step is to identify your career goals. Are you interested in quantum computing, quantum communication, quantum sensing, or a combination thereof? Do you want to work in research, development, consulting, or entrepreneurship? Are you drawn to a particular industry, like biotech, finance, or cybersecurity? Be clear about your interests, your strengths, and your aspirations.

With your career goals in mind, it's time to develop the necessary skills. Quantum technologies demand a diverse skillset, blending physics, computer science, engineering, mathematics, and more. Depending on your goals, you might need to delve into quantum mechanics, quantum algorithms, quantum error correction, or quantum information theory.

There are a plethora of resources available for learning these skills, from university courses and online platforms to textbooks and scientific papers. Choose learning resources that match your learning style, your budget, and your schedule. Remember, acquiring these skills is not a sprint, but a marathon; it requires patience, practice, and perseverance.

A unique aspect of the quantum field is the importance of hands-on experience. Quantum technologies are not just theoretical – they're practical and experimental. Gaining hands-on experience with quantum systems, be it through laboratory work, internships, or projects, is invaluable. There are also online platforms that provide access to quantum computers, enabling you to run your own quantum programs and learn by doing.

Another crucial step in the quantum job hunt is building your network. The quantum field, while rapidly growing, is still relatively small and close-knit. Networking can open doors to opportunities, provide valuable insights, and offer support and mentorship. Attend quantum-related events, join quantum societies or online communities, and connect with quantum professionals on platforms like LinkedIn.

When it comes to job hunting, be proactive and strategic. Don't just rely on job boards; reach out to companies, labs, or institutes that you're interested in, even if they don't have open positions. Tailor your application to each role, highlighting your relevant skills, experiences, and passion for quantum technologies. In your interviews, show your enthusiasm, your curiosity, and your readiness to learn and grow.

It's also important to keep up with the latest developments in the quantum field. Quantum technologies are advancing rapidly, and staying updated can give you a competitive edge. Follow quantum news, read recent scientific papers, and engage in discussions about the latest breakthroughs. This will not only benefit your job hunt but also fuel your continuous learning in the field.

Finally, be resilient and persistent. The quantum job hunt can be challenging and unpredictable, given the nascent and dynamic nature of the field. You might face setbacks, rejections, or uncertainties. But remember, every challenge is an opportunity to learn, adapt, and become stronger. Keep your goals in sight, and stay committed to your journey in the quantum field.

Mapping out your future career in the quantum field involves understanding the landscape, defining your goals, developing the necessary skills, gaining hands-on experience, building your network, being proactive in your job hunt, staying updated, and showing resilience. Each step is an integral part of your quantum career journey, contributing to your growth and success in the field. With this roadmap, you're well-equipped to navigate the quantum job hunt and make your mark in the quantum revolution.

Chapter 8: Quantum Meets AI: A New Synergy

When Quantum Computing and AI Collide: A Powerful Partnership

As we cross the threshold into the quantum age, two disruptive technologies are on a collision course - Artificial Intelligence (AI) and Quantum Computing. When these potent forces combine, they promise to revolutionize myriad sectors, from healthcare and materials science to cryptography and machine learning. The merging of AI and Quantum Computing is not just another tech trend; it's a dynamic alliance that could unlock capabilities we've only begun to imagine.

At the heart of this convergence is the power of quantum computers to process vast amounts of information incredibly fast, solving complex problems that today's computers would take centuries to crack. AI, with its ability to learn from data and make intelligent decisions, can be turbocharged by the exponential processing power of quantum computing. In essence, AI can help us make sense of the quantum world, and quantum computing can help AI reach new heights of intelligence and capability.
Let's delve a little deeper into what happens when Quantum Computing and AI collide and how this powerful partnership might shape the future.

Quantum Computing is driven by the principles of quantum mechanics, enabling it to solve complex problems at an unprecedented speed. This power can be harnessed to speed up machine learning algorithms - a subset of AI that enables systems to learn from data, identify patterns, and make decisions. Currently, large-scale machine learning tasks are computationally intensive, requiring enormous power and time. Quantum computers, however, could perform these tasks with ease and speed, enabling quicker and more accurate insights.

In recent years, the concept of Quantum Machine Learning (QML) has emerged, combining quantum algorithms with machine learning techniques to create faster, more efficient learning systems. Quantum versions of neural networks, called quantum neural networks (QNNs), are being developed, potentially leading to more powerful and efficient AI models.

On the flip side, AI can help us harness the power of Quantum Computing. Quantum systems are notoriously tricky to understand and control. However, AI, with its ability to analyze complex systems and learn from data, can help us manage and optimize quantum systems. For instance, AI can be used to correct errors in quantum computations, which is one of the biggest challenges in developing practical quantum computers.

Quantum technologies also hold promise for advancing AI's capabilities. One of the hurdles for AI development is the 'curse of dimensionality,' a problem that arises when analyzing and visualizing high-dimensional data. Quantum systems, however, naturally live in high-dimensional spaces, potentially giving AI the ability to handle complex, multi-dimensional data more efficiently.

There's a real sense of excitement about the potential of the AI and Quantum Computing partnership, but it's not without its challenges. Quantum computers are still in their infancy, with noise and errors posing significant obstacles to their practical use. Moreover, developing quantum algorithms for machine learning tasks is a complex task, requiring a deep understanding of both fields.

To overcome these challenges and reap the benefits of this potent combination, we need a robust research and development ecosystem. This includes investment in quantum technologies, interdisciplinary collaborations, and education programs to train a new generation of quantum-AI specialists. Policymakers, researchers, and industry leaders need to work together to guide the responsible development and use of these technologies, addressing issues like ethics, privacy, and security.

The convergence of Quantum Computing and AI opens up a world of possibilities. This potent partnership can transform machine learning, optimize quantum systems, and solve complex problems, paving the way for breakthroughs in various sectors. The road ahead may be fraught with challenges, but the rewards promise to be game-changing, making this a journey worth undertaking.

As we continue to navigate this uncharted territory, remember that the goal isn't just technological advancement, but creating a future that benefits all of humanity. With a commitment to ethical principles, collaborative efforts, and continuous learning, we can harness the power of Quantum Computing and AI to shape a future that's not just technologically advanced, but also sustainable, inclusive, and prosperous.

Quantum-Boosted AI: Surpassing Limitations of Classic Computing

The marriage of quantum computing and artificial intelligence is expected to bring about a seismic shift in the technological landscape. Their synergy promises to eclipse the limitations of classical computing, granting us new ways to process information and solve complex problems. As we proceed through this epoch of digital metamorphosis, it's essential to explore how this alliance can help us transcend the constraints we face today.

Quantum computing harnesses the peculiar properties of quantum mechanics, like superposition and entanglement, allowing it to process vast amounts of information simultaneously. In stark contrast, classical computers work with bits that can either be in a state of 0 or 1, whereas quantum bits or qubits can be in a state of 0, 1, or both at the same time due to superposition. This fundamental difference grants quantum computers immense computational power that can be harnessed to tackle problems deemed insurmountable for classical systems.

Simultaneously, AI's learning algorithms are transforming industries by making systems more intelligent. However, many AI models, particularly those involved in deep learning, are computationally intensive and require a great deal of time and resources to train. They can take days or even weeks to process complex datasets on classical machines.

That's where the combination of quantum computing and AI comes into play. Quantum computing's exponential computational power can drastically speed up AI's data processing ability, breaking down barriers that currently limit its applications. With quantum-boosted AI, we can make predictions and inferences from colossal datasets within a fraction of the time classical computers require, accelerating the pace of discovery and innovation.

For instance, quantum-boosted AI could have transformative impacts in the field of healthcare. Training machine learning models with massive datasets to predict disease patterns, personalized treatments, and drug interactions is a slow and challenging process on classical machines. But quantum computing could accelerate this process, leading to quicker diagnoses and personalized treatments, potentially saving countless lives.

In the realm of finance, quantum-boosted AI can optimize portfolio management by analyzing numerous variables and potential scenarios in an instant, offering far better financial predictions and risk assessments than possible today.

The challenge we face in leveraging the full potential of quantum-boosted AI lies in quantum hardware's current stage of development. Quantum systems are susceptible to noise and errors, limiting the reliability and scalability of these systems. However, through a continual cycle of research, development, and testing, these challenges can be surmounted.

Simultaneously, developing quantum algorithms compatible with machine learning tasks is a complex endeavor requiring a deep understanding of quantum mechanics, computer science, and data analytics. It calls for multidisciplinary collaboration and knowledge-sharing among experts in these fields.

There's another significant challenge in the form of quantum programming. Quantum computers use a different set of rules compared to their classical counterparts. As such, we need quantum programmers who understand these rules to build quantum algorithms. Currently, there's a shortage of professionals with these skills, underscoring the need for quantum education and training programs.

The road to quantum-boosted AI might be challenging, but it's an exciting journey that promises to change the world as we know it. The sheer potential of this technology, from creating powerful AI models to cracking complex problems in science and medicine, presents a compelling case for investment and research in this field.

Moreover, this isn't just about embracing advanced technology. It's about how we use that technology to create a brighter future. Quantum-boosted AI can be a tool to tackle some of humanity's most pressing challenges, from climate change to healthcare disparities. However, we must ensure that as we develop these technologies, we do so ethically and responsibly.

Quantum-boosted AI is a powerful force that can surpass the limitations of classical computing, paving the way for breakthroughs we're only beginning to envision. The journey toward this future will require continued investment in research and development, fostering multidisciplinary collaborations, and building a skilled workforce ready to drive the quantum revolution. With the right strategies and commitment, we can navigate the challenges and seize the opportunities that quantum-boosted AI presents, shaping a future where technology serves humanity's best interests.

The Future of Learning Machines: Quantum Algorithms in Action

The field of artificial intelligence has been redefined by machine learning, wherein machines learn from data, identifying patterns, making decisions, and improving their performance over time without being explicitly programmed to do so. However, the scale and complexity of data now available pose challenges that strain the processing capabilities of classical computers. Enter quantum computing, and we have a revolution on our hands.

Quantum computing, exploiting the rules of quantum mechanics, introduces a new level of processing power that could potentially transform the field of machine learning. But how do quantum algorithms fit into this narrative, and what does it mean for the future of learning machines? Let's delve into this exciting frontier.

In the world of quantum computing, quantum algorithms are the crucial cog that sets the machine in motion. A quantum algorithm is a step-by-step procedure, where each step involves quantum operations – manipulating quantum data to solve a particular problem. Quantum algorithms, such as Shor's algorithm for factorizing large numbers and Grover's algorithm for searching databases, have demonstrated theoretical advantages over classical algorithms. This power can be harnessed to tackle complex machine learning problems more efficiently and in ways previously not possible.

To appreciate this quantum edge in machine learning, consider how a quantum computer would approach a complex problem. Traditional machine learning relies on classical computers that process information sequentially, which can be time-consuming with large datasets.

However, a quantum computer uses quantum bits or 'qubits,' which, due to quantum superposition, can represent multiple states simultaneously. As a result, quantum computers can process a vast number of potential outcomes at the same time.

For machine learning, this equates to an exponential increase in processing power, leading to faster training times for models and enabling the analysis of larger, more complex datasets. For instance, a quantum algorithm known as Quantum Support Vector Machine (QSVM) can potentially speed up the training process for a type of machine learning model called the support vector machine.

However, quantum algorithms and quantum machine learning are still nascent fields, and many challenges need to be addressed to realize their full potential.

Quantum hardware is still in its early stages, and current quantum computers, often referred to as Noisy Intermediate-Scale Quantum (NISQ) devices, are susceptible to errors and noise, limiting their reliability. While error correction and noise reduction techniques are in development, it will take time and significant research efforts to build stable, large-scale quantum computers.

Furthermore, creating quantum algorithms suitable for machine learning tasks requires a deep understanding of both quantum physics and machine learning. It calls for an unprecedented level of interdisciplinary cooperation among physicists, computer scientists, and data scientists. The pool of professionals with expertise in both these areas is currently quite limited.

To bridge this gap, the education sector needs to evolve, introducing programs that provide an integrated approach to learning about quantum computing and machine learning. Institutions must foster environments that encourage interdisciplinary learning and collaboration. Meanwhile, industries should invest in training programs to upskill their workforce, preparing them for the quantum revolution that is to come.

Another hurdle is the theoretical nature of many aspects of quantum machine learning. Much of the quantum advantage in machine learning is currently theoretical, with practical demonstrations lagging due to hardware limitations. Future research should focus on converting these theoretical advantages into practical applications, which could mean finding ways to implement quantum algorithms on NISQ devices or developing novel quantum algorithms specifically designed for these devices.

As these challenges are addressed, the potential applications of quantum algorithms in machine learning are vast and exciting. In healthcare, quantum algorithms could help machine learning models analyze complex biological data to predict disease progression, discover new drugs, or personalize treatment plans. In climate science, they could analyze complex climate models to make accurate predictions about climate change. In finance, they could help analyze market trends and make predictions with unprecedented accuracy.

The intersection of quantum computing and machine learning heralds a promising future for learning machines. Quantum algorithms could vastly enhance the computational power of machine learning, opening up new opportunities and applications. However, realizing this potential will require continued investment in quantum hardware development, education and training, and interdisciplinary research. As we navigate this journey, the goal should always be to harness quantum technology's power to solve real-world problems and make a positive impact on society.

Quantum AI: Rethinking Intelligent Systems and Automation

The Quantum Age is anticipated to overhaul our existing technological and societal infrastructures, and one area where it promises significant disruption is artificial intelligence (AI). The melding of quantum computing and AI, a field now called Quantum AI, invites us to rethink the entire landscape of intelligent systems and automation.

At present, our AI systems are grounded on classical computing, which, despite its remarkable progress, still suffers from inherent limitations. For instance, processing large volumes of data or simulating complex systems like weather patterns and biological systems strain classical computers. The advent of quantum computing, with its potential for unparalleled computational power, is an invitation to revolutionize AI, advancing its capability to handle complex tasks, thus redefining intelligent systems and automation.

So, what is Quantum AI, and why does it promise such a revolution?

Quantum AI combines quantum computing's principles with AI's machine learning algorithms, providing a powerful symbiotic relationship. Quantum computing, with its ability to compute multiple possibilities simultaneously through superposition, provides the potential for a seismic acceleration in the processing power available for machine learning algorithms.

The implications of this fusion of quantum computing and AI are profound and far-reaching. We're looking at the prospect of building intelligent systems capable of deciphering large datasets in a fraction of the time required by classical computers, potentially opening up new avenues in fields like genomics, climate modeling, drug discovery, and more.

Furthermore, Quantum AI could significantly advance automation, where tasks are increasingly performed by machines, software, or algorithms. Quantum-enhanced machine learning could handle more complex tasks, make better predictions, and adapt more quickly to changes in data. This could revolutionize industries where automation plays a significant role, such as manufacturing, logistics, healthcare, and finance, driving unprecedented levels of efficiency and innovation.

However, as with any revolutionary technology, Quantum AI comes with its own set of challenges and considerations, which we need to address to leverage its potential fully.

One of the main challenges is the current state of quantum hardware. Quantum computers are still in their infancy, with only a few qubits available for computations that are susceptible to errors. The path to developing reliable, large-scale quantum computers is a complex and challenging journey. Continuous investment in quantum technology, encouraging collaboration among researchers, governments, and industries, and fostering an ecosystem that supports the development of quantum hardware is crucial.

Another major challenge lies in the development of quantum machine learning algorithms. Classical machine learning algorithms cannot be directly implemented on quantum computers; they need to be translated into quantum versions. Moreover, not all problems will benefit from a quantum approach, so discerning where quantum advantages can be leveraged will be crucial.

This task calls for a new breed of professionals skilled in quantum mechanics, AI, and machine learning – a tall order given the current education and training landscape. It necessitates a rethinking of our educational systems to foster cross-disciplinary learning, bridging physics with computer science, and AI with quantum mechanics.

Now, let's think about the societal implications of Quantum AI. With the promise of more powerful AI systems and advanced automation, how we work and live could be fundamentally changed. Jobs could be displaced, and new types of jobs could be created, necessitating a massive reskilling and upskilling effort. Public policy, education, and industry practices need to evolve to prepare for and mitigate these disruptions, ensuring that the benefits of Quantum AI are equitably distributed.

The ethical and privacy considerations of Quantum AI are also critical. With more powerful AI comes the risk of misuse. The governance of Quantum AI, involving clear guidelines, regulations, and oversight, is essential to prevent unethical use, ensure privacy, and build public trust in these advanced technologies.

Quantum AI invites us to rethink the future of intelligent systems and automation, offering remarkable potential but also posing significant challenges and ethical considerations. To navigate this new frontier successfully, a comprehensive and collaborative approach is needed, involving advancements in quantum technology, cross-disciplinary education, responsible governance, and inclusive public policy. With such an approach, we can look forward to a future where Quantum AI drives innovation and progress while respecting our values and enhancing our societal well-being.

Chapter 9: Conclusion: Embracing the Quantum Future

The Quantum Revolution Impact: A New Era of Technology and Innovation

As we conclude our exploration of quantum frontiers, it's important to remember that we're standing at the threshold of a new era. The quantum revolution is about more than just a surge in computational power or the ability to accurately simulate quantum phenomena; it's about ushering in a new age of technology and innovation, the full impact of which we can only begin to fathom.

In an increasingly digital world, computational power is the cornerstone of innovation and progress. We rely on it to design efficient logistical networks, make accurate weather predictions, develop new materials, and decipher the mysteries of our DNA. However, despite the undeniable power of classical computers, they still struggle with many of these tasks. The quantum revolution promises to overcome these obstacles, rendering previously intractable problems within our reach and providing us with unprecedented insights into the nature of reality itself.

To fully comprehend the impact of the quantum revolution, we must consider its potential in various fields. In healthcare, quantum computing could help us model complex biochemical reactions, opening the doors to new drug discovery and personalized medicine. In logistics and supply chains, quantum optimization algorithms could enable us to find the most efficient solutions, saving time and resources. In the fight against climate change, quantum computing could help us design new materials for carbon capture or optimize renewable energy grids.

Moreover, the fusion of quantum computing with artificial intelligence – the emerging field of Quantum AI – is poised to redefine the landscape of intelligent systems and automation. We're looking at the prospect of intelligent systems that can decipher larger datasets in a fraction of the time required by classical computers, transforming industries like genomics, climate modeling, drug discovery, and more.

Yet, as we stand on the cusp of this quantum revolution, it's important to acknowledge that this journey will not be without its challenges. The hardware is still maturing, and error correction is a significant hurdle. Quantum algorithms are in their infancy, and developing new ones is a complex process that requires expertise in both quantum mechanics and computer science.

There's also a pressing need for quantum-skilled talent. The quantum revolution demands a new breed of professionals who are versed in quantum mechanics, computer science, and AI. This calls for a transformation in our education systems, encouraging cross-disciplinary learning and fostering an environment that inspires the quantum pioneers of tomorrow.

The societal implications of the quantum revolution will be far-reaching, influencing the job market, public policy, and our daily lives. We must prepare for this quantum future, ensuring that public policy, education, and industry practices evolve to harness the potential of quantum technologies while addressing the disruptions they may cause.

Furthermore, the ethical implications of quantum technologies must be considered. Quantum encryption could provide unparalleled data security, but it could also make certain cryptographic systems obsolete, posing challenges for data privacy and national security. We must build governance structures for quantum technologies, ensuring that they're used responsibly and ethically.

Embracing the quantum future involves more than simply welcoming the technological advancements it promises. It requires a holistic approach, balancing the technological progress with societal, educational, and ethical considerations. It calls for collaboration between scientists, policymakers, educators, and the public. Only by doing so can we ensure that the quantum revolution ushers in not just a new era of technology and innovation, but a future that enhances our societal wellbeing and upholds our shared values.

The quantum revolution is more than just a chapter in the history of technology; it's the beginning of a new narrative – one in which the principles of the quantum world shape our technologies, our societies, and our future. And while the quantum frontier may be vast and unexplored, it's a journey worth embarking on. For it's in exploring these new frontiers that we unlock new possibilities, push the boundaries of what's achievable, and, ultimately, shape the future we want to live in.

Quantum Mechanics Future Technology: Predictions and Possibilities

The crystal ball of technology has always been a kaleidoscope of intriguing possibilities, and with quantum mechanics taking center stage, the images coming into focus are even more fascinating. As we peer into the future of quantum technology, we must realize that this journey into the 'quantum realm' is not just about enhancing computational speed or even about overcoming the limitations of classical physics. It's about stepping into a realm of new possibilities, where the rules of the game are fundamentally different.

The field of quantum mechanics, with its inherent uncertainty and strange phenomena like entanglement and superposition, has perplexed and intrigued scientists for over a century. Yet, it is these very phenomena that hold the key to a future powered by quantum technology. The potential impact is far-reaching and could extend to areas as diverse as cryptography, material science, artificial intelligence, medicine, and more.

Let's start with quantum computing. The concept of a quantum computer leverages quantum bits or qubits, which unlike their classical counterparts, can be in a superposition of states, allowing quantum computers to handle a vast amount of information simultaneously. This could result in a seismic shift in computational power, allowing us to solve problems considered too complex or time-consuming for classical computers.

Take, for instance, the field of medicine. Drug discovery is a notoriously long and complex process, largely due to the difficulty of simulating the quantum behavior of molecules. With quantum computers, we could efficiently model molecular interactions, significantly speeding up the process of discovering new drugs and personalized treatments.

Quantum computing also has potential implications for artificial intelligence. By facilitating faster and more complex calculations, quantum computing could aid the development of more advanced machine learning algorithms, allowing AI to analyze bigger datasets, make more accurate predictions, and optimize complex systems more efficiently. This could transform fields ranging from climate modeling to logistics to financial analysis.

But the potential of quantum mechanics extends beyond just quantum computing. The principles of quantum mechanics are also paving the way for quantum communication and quantum cryptography. Quantum communication leverages the principle of quantum entanglement to transmit information in a completely secure manner. This could revolutionize the field of data security, offering a way to communicate that's immune to eavesdropping.

In parallel, quantum cryptography, specifically quantum key distribution (QKD), utilizes the properties of quantum mechanics to create uncrackable encryption keys. Given the increasing importance of cybersecurity in our digital age, quantum cryptography could play a critical role in safeguarding our data and communications in the future.

Quantum sensors represent another area of immense potential. Leveraging quantum phenomena, these sensors could measure physical quantities like temperature, pressure, or magnetic fields with unprecedented precision. This could have applications ranging from navigation to medical imaging to detecting gravitational waves.

As we gaze into the future of quantum technology, it's crucial to note that the road ahead is not without its challenges. Quantum systems are incredibly delicate, and maintaining their quantum states is no easy feat. Errors are currently a major obstacle, requiring sophisticated error correction techniques. We also need to cultivate a workforce skilled in quantum mechanics to further this field and maximize its potential.

As we stand at the precipice of the quantum future, we need to be mindful of these challenges and proactive in addressing them. But despite these hurdles, the possibilities that quantum mechanics offers are too compelling to ignore. As physicist Richard Feynman once said, "Nature isn't classical, dammit, and if you want to make a simulation of nature, you'd better make it quantum mechanical."

Indeed, the quantum revolution is more than a technological upheaval. It's a fundamental shift in our understanding of the world and how we can harness its rules to drive innovation and progress. As we continue to decipher the quantum realm, we will likely unlock possibilities we can't yet imagine, propelling us into a future where the lines between science fiction and reality blur.

The quantum future is a landscape of vast potential, teeming with possibilities as intriguing as the quantum world itself. It's a future that promises to redefine the realms of computation, communication, and sensing, opening doors to innovations that could transform our societies and our lives.

The path to the quantum future is illuminated by the fascinating and strange light of quantum mechanics. It's a path that leads us into uncharted territory, filled with challenges but also immense potential. Embracing the quantum future means being open to new paradigms, fostering cross-disciplinary collaborations, and nurturing a new generation of quantum-literate professionals. It's a journey towards a future that's not merely an iteration of the present but a leap into a new realm of possibilities, shaped by the fundamental principles of the quantum world.

Quantum Frontiers: The Continual Journey into the Quantum Realm

As we embark on a new era of technological progress defined by quantum mechanics, we're stepping into a journey that will continually expand our understanding of the universe and how we interact with it. This is the ever-unfolding narrative of the quantum frontier - a tale of exploration, discovery, and ingenuity that will play out in the decades to come.

The quantum realm, characterized by superposition, entanglement, and inherent uncertainty, is fundamentally different from our classical world. But as we delve deeper into this realm, we're discovering ways to harness these quantum phenomena to create technology that has the potential to reshape our world. From quantum computing and cryptography to quantum sensing and communication, the array of possibilities is incredibly vast and exciting.

The quantum journey has already begun with the development of quantum computers. While still in the early stages, quantum computers, with their ability to process enormous amounts of data simultaneously, hold the promise of revolutionizing fields as diverse as cryptography, logistics, drug discovery, and more.

The ongoing development of quantum algorithms to optimize these quantum machines is an integral part of this journey. As we continue to push the boundaries of our computational abilities, we're not just advancing technology but also enhancing our understanding of quantum mechanics itself. In a sense, every quantum algorithm we design and every qubit we manipulate is a step further into the quantum frontier.

Simultaneously, the quest for quantum supremacy – the point at which a quantum computer can perform a task that's practically impossible for a classical computer – is an ongoing narrative. Achieving quantum supremacy isn't just about computational might; it's about proving the practical utility of quantum mechanics in real-world applications. It's a crucial milestone on our quantum journey, and one that's drawing ever closer.

The journey into the quantum realm is also pushing us into uncharted territory in communication and security. Quantum communication, underpinned by the phenomenon of quantum entanglement, holds the promise of completely secure communication channels. Meanwhile, quantum cryptography, through techniques such as quantum key distribution, is paving the way for virtually uncrackable codes. As our digital world continues to expand, these technologies could play a vital role in safeguarding our data.

Alongside these developments, the potential of quantum sensing is being explored. By harnessing quantum effects, we could create sensors with unprecedented precision, with applications ranging from medical imaging to navigation systems and gravitational wave detection.

As we navigate the quantum frontier, it's important to remember that we're not just passengers on this journey; we're explorers. And like all explorers, we will face challenges and obstacles. Quantum systems are notoriously delicate, and maintaining their coherence is a significant hurdle. Plus, the principles of quantum mechanics are still not fully understood, leaving us with many questions to answer.

Yet, these challenges also represent opportunities for discovery and innovation. As we tackle the obstacles in our path, we'll deepen our understanding of quantum mechanics, spurring further advancements in quantum technology.

Moreover, our quantum journey is not a solo venture. It requires a collaborative, multidisciplinary effort involving physicists, computer scientists, engineers, and even philosophers. We'll need to educate a new generation of quantum-literate professionals who can contribute to and navigate this quantum world.

We must also consider the societal implications of our journey into the quantum realm. With any new technology, there are potential ethical, privacy, and security issues. It's vital to have these conversations early and to include a wide range of voices in them.

The continual journey into the quantum realm is undoubtedly complex, but it's also incredibly exciting. It's a journey that will continue to expand our horizons, unlocking new possibilities for technology and reshaping our understanding of the universe. With each step we take into the quantum frontier, we're not just making technological progress; we're participating in a grand scientific adventure.

In the end, our journey into the quantum frontier is more than just an exploration of new technological possibilities; it's a quest for knowledge, an adventure that pushes us to expand our understanding of the universe. It's a testament to human curiosity, ingenuity, and our never-ending pursuit of progress. And while we may not know exactly what lies ahead, we can be sure that our quantum journey will continue to be an exciting, challenging, and transformative one.

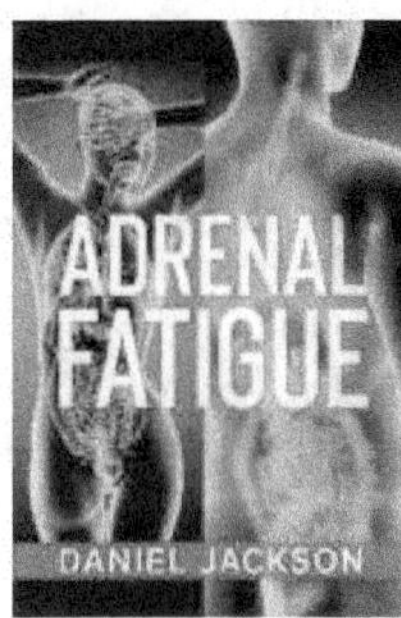

Take a look at more great books available from Rockwood Publishing

... some for FREE!

Just visit the link below:

rockwoodpublishing.co.uk

to the subject matter covered. The information included in this book has been compiled to give an overview of the subject(s) and detail some of the symptoms, treatments etc. that are available to people with this condition. It is not intended to give medical advice. For a firm diagnosis of your condition, and for a treatment plan suitable for you, you should consult your doctor or consultant. The writer of this book and the publisher are not responsible for any damages or negative consequences following any of the treatments or methods highlighted in this book. Website links are for informational purposes and should not be seen as a personal endorsement; the same applies to the products detailed in this book. The reader should also be aware that although the web links included were correct at the time of writing, they may become out of date in the future.

Disclaimers

The content contained within this book is for information and entertainment purposes only, and in no way purports to represent professional medical opinion. It should NOT be used as a substitute for expert advice, and you must consult with your designated health professional before acting upon any information contained herein or before undertaking any practice whose methodology is referred to in this book. The author is NOT a registered health professional and the text merely represents personal opinion, not medical fact. The author cannot be held responsible for the consequences of any action derived from the reading of this book, as the content is not based on diagnosis and subsequent regimen. It is the reader's responsibility to seek proper, professional medical advice from a registered health practitioner in connection with any material contained within this book.

Legal Disclaimer (part 1)

Nothing in this book should be construed as an attempt to diagnose, treat or cure. The information in this book is intended to be a community resource. The author takes no responsibility for any informational material or brochures produced using information taken from this book. The author has endeavoured to ensure that all information is correct at the time of publication. This information, however, is subject to change without notice. The author makes no warranty with regard to the accuracy of any information and will not be liable for any errors or omissions. Any liability that arises as a result of this information is hereby excluded to the fullest extent allowed by law.

This information should not be used as a substitute for seeking independent professional advice.

Legal Disclaimer (part 2)

Disclaimer and Terms of Use:

a) i. In publishing this information, the author makes no representations concerning the efficacy, appropriateness or suitability of any products or treatments. Use this information at your own risk. The compiler is not a doctor and has no medical background or training.

ii. Statements and information regarding dietary supplements, books and any products mentioned have not been evaluated by any health authority and are not intended to diagnose, treat, cure or prevent any disease or health condition.

b) In view of the possibility of human error, neither the author nor any other party involved in providing this information, warrant that the information contained therein is in every respect accurate or complete and they are not responsible nor liable for any errors or omissions that may be found or for the results obtained from the use of such information. The entire risk as to use of this information is assumed by the user.

c) You are encouraged to consult other sources and confirm the information.

d) The information you access is provided "as is". No warranty, expressed or implied, is given as to the accuracy, completeness or timeliness of any information herein, or for obtaining legal advice. To the fullest extent permissible pursuant to applicable law, neither the author nor any other parties who have been involved in the creation, preparation, printing, or delivering of this information assume responsibility for the completeness, accuracy, timeliness, errors or omissions of said information and assume no liability for any direct, incidental, consequential, indirect, or punitive damages as well as any circumstance for any complication, injuries, side effects or other medical accidents to person or property arising from or in connection with the use or reliance upon any information contained herein.

e) The author is not responsible for the contents of any linked site or any link contained in a linked site, or any changes or update to such sites. The inclusion of any link does not imply endorsement by the author. The author makes no representations or claims as to the quality, content and accuracy of the information, services, products, messages which may be provided by such resources, and specifically disclaims any warranties, including but not limited to implied or express warranties of merchantability or fitness for any particular usage, application or purpose.

f) The information provided is general in nature and is intended for educational and informational purposes only. It is not intended to replace or substitute the evaluation, judgment, diagnosis, and medical or preventative care of a physician, paediatrician, therapist and/or health care provider.

g) Any medical, nutritional, dietetic, therapeutic or other decisions, dosages, treatments or drug regimes should be made in consultation with a health care practitioner. Do not discontinue treatment or medication without first consulting your physician, clinician or therapist.

h) By reading this information, you signify your assent to these terms and conditions of use. If you do not agree to these terms and conditions of use, do not read/use this information. If any provision of these terms and conditions of use shall be determined to be unlawful, void or for any reason unenforceable, then that provision shall be deemed severable from this agreement and shall not affect the validity and enforceability of any remaining provisions.

i) The information, services, products, messages and other materials, individually and collectively, are provided with the understanding that the author is not engaged in rendering medical advice or recommendations.

j) The information and the terms of use are subject to change without notice. The material provided as is without warranty of any kind and may include inaccuracies and/or typographical errors. The author makes no representations about the suitability of this information for any purpose. The author disclaims all warranties with regard to this information, including all implied warranties, and in no event shall the author be held liable, resulting from, or in any way related to, the use of this information.

k) The unauthorized alteration of the content of this information is expressly prohibited. The author, its agents and representatives shall not be responsible for any claims, actions or damages which may arise on account of the unauthorized alteration of this information.

www.ingramcontent.com/pod-product-compliance
Lightning Source LLC
Chambersburg PA
CBHW071328150726
47997CB00002B/637